D0438105

YOUR BUSINESS
YOUR FAMILY
THEIR FUTURE

Emily Griffiths-Hamilton

— YOUR —
BUSINESS
— YOUR —
FAMILY
— THEIR —
FUTURE

How to Ensure Your Family Enterprise Thrives for Generations

Figure.1

Vancouver / Berkeley

Cataloguing data is available from Library and Archives Canada
ISBN 978-1-77327-053-1 (hbk.)
ISBN 978-1-77327-054-8 (ebook)
ISBN 978-1-77327-055-5 (pdf)

Editing by Barbara Pulling
Copy editing by Lesley Cameron
Proofreading by Renate Preuss
Indexing by Stephen Ullstrom

Design by Jessica Sullivan
Author photograph by Marc Dionne Reactive Design Inc.

Printed and bound in Canada by Friesens
Distributed in the U.S. by Publishers Group West

Figure 1 Publishing Inc.
Vancouver BC Canada
www.figure1publishing.com

To my husband, Paul,
and our sons, David and Brandon,

For all that you have been,
all that you are,
and all that you will be.
Each and every day, I am grateful
for our shared journey.

I treasure you all.

CONTENTS

FOREWORD

I HAVE KNOWN Emily and her family for decades—Boston Pizza was one of the first tenants in GM Place, the Vancouver arena that she and her partners financed, built and operated. I've seen her build and lead a high-profile family enterprise, and then focus her considerable education, training and experience to help other family enterprises reach their goals.

Your Business, Your Family, Their Future is loaded with insights that are presented clearly and concisely. Emily tackles important topics with deep knowledge and first-hand understanding: how to deal with the potential struggle of "letting go"; successfully incorporating your family members into your business; working with unhappy or unqualified family members; making decisions while balancing the voting rights of family members, and many more.

There is value here for anyone involved with a private business of any kind, at any stage. This is a book you'll want to keep around. In fact, this is a book I'll keep coming back to. What an exciting read!

JIM TRELIVING
Chairman and owner, Boston Pizza International
Personality on CBC's *The Dragon's Den*

INTRODUCTION:
Put Your Family
on the Path to Success

THERE IS NO institution more enduring than the family business. Family businesses predate multinational corporations, the Industrial Revolution, the Enlightenment and even the Roman Empire. According to the Family Firm Institute, family businesses—businesses in which decision-making is influenced by a family—constitute between 70% and 90% of GDP annually and create 50%–80% of jobs in the majority of countries worldwide today. That makes family businesses economic powerhouses that drive local, national and global economies. For every high-profile family business like Ford, Walmart, The New York Times, Lavazza, Tata, Kikkoman, Taittinger and Samsung, there are thousands of lower-profile, private family-owned businesses making decisions about how to manage and grow their operations. In this book, I'll share my insights about what successful families know and how they leverage that knowledge to remain strong across multiple generations.

A vast body of knowledge has been generated by business scholars and researchers investigating how successful family enterprises remain robust across generations. My goal is to consolidate this information, giving you and your family a useful entry point for building a multigenerational family enterprise. I'll also share suggestions, tips and strategies based on the common patterns found within successful families.

To do this, I've drawn on personal experience, extensive independent research and years of work as a family enterprise advisor, a family business advisory board member and a family meeting facilitator. Growing up, I had a ringside seat at the family business table of my visionary maternal grandfather, veterinarian Dr. William Ballard. During the Great Depression, my grandfather came up with what turned out to be a wildly popular formula for dog food and then, in a revolutionary move, canned it for easier distribution. As the youngest of his many grandchildren, I grew up with first-hand knowledge of the workings of the family business and the results of its transition of ownership.

My father was also a visionary business builder and leader. Alongside his highly respected career as a chartered accountant (CA) in public practice, he built a media and sports empire that ultimately spanned radio, television and satellite communications across Canada and the ownership of our community's beloved National Hockey League team, the Vancouver Canucks. Although I was the youngest of four siblings, I had a front-row, fully participating family-member seat at the table. The insights I gained in the years that followed came from the perspective of being the only sibling in my family to obtain a professional designation, as a CA, and to work entirely independently of my family.

As a member of the third generation, I became a decision maker, a role entirely different from simply having a seat at the table. The ownership group I belonged to—which included one of my brothers, Arthur Griffiths, and John and Bruce McCaw—bought the Vancouver Canucks, financed the construction of a state-of-the-art arena in the city of Vancouver and bought the Vancouver Grizzlies, one of the first two National Basketball Association (NBA) franchises awarded in Canada. That was a wild, all-consuming roller coaster ride. At a certain point, I made the decision to sell my interest in the sports and entertainment holdings and to reformat our family enterprise's financial assets into the financial markets and direct real estate holdings and build our Family Office. Now into its fourth generation, our family enterprise continues to evolve and flourish.

In the decades over which my career developed, I began to focus on the topic of how successful family enterprises thrive for generations. As a CA working with other families who, like my own, had used the traditional tax- and control-driven tools to deal with family enterprise transitions, resulting in complex family corporate structures that often included trusts and holdcos, and later, as a family enterprise advisor, I started to see that successful families shared a number of traits. However, in so much of the information flooding the market on the subject of successful multigenerational family enterprises, these traits seemed lost in a sea of unnecessary complications.

Here's one example. I receive regular emails from different sources on the latest research into family enterprises. A recent one caught my attention because of its vibrantly colored diagram: elongated oval shapes that overlapped and fanned out like the feathers on a peacock. Each tiny overlapping area was labeled with a different acronym: fifteen of them in total. Following the website link, I discovered this complex model existed to explain the role of "governance" in a family enterprise. I shared the link with a business owner who responded, "Wow! I can't get my kids out of bed in the morning. How am I going to get through all this?" In this book, you will discover that the work required to make your family enterprise thrive isn't complicated.

For instance, the topic of family business "governance" in family enterprises implies the need for a complex, rigid structure, but that runs contrary to the trait that has made most business builders successful: their ability to be adaptable and flexible. For that reason, I use the term "family enterprise framework" instead. Successful family enterprises know that it's important to create a family enterprise framework that's both flexible and solid enough to allow for sound decisions to be made when there are many decision makers in later generations, which in turn allows your family enterprise to evolve and thrive for many generations to come.

Many family business builders and owners are already living very busy professional and personal lives, and they want to know how much work and time will be required to ensure their family enterprise remains robust across multiple generations. This book addresses that question by walking you through the steps required and showing how each generation will share in the lifting. In fact, you'll discover that your family enterprise will be strengthened when family members share the work to be done.

The traditional approaches to multigenerational family business transition lose sight of the most powerful element in any family business: a united family. While every family is unique, there are common traits to be found in the long-term journeys of sustainable family enterprises. The work you and your family do together to articulate your shared values and vision, establish a dynamic family enterprise framework and create effective, agreed-upon decision-making processes and policies will help position your family enterprise to make the best possible decisions going into the future. By working together, you will also strengthen family bonds of trust and unity across generations.

As I note in my earlier book, *Build Your Family Bank*, passion is a key element in any successful family business. When a family enterprise flourishes across many generations, the passion required to succeed can arise in any of the three family enterprise systems: the family, family business ownership or family business management. Because family members are increasingly mobile, less bound by place and less tied to life-long careers, a multigenerational family enterprise can offer community and connectedness in an increasingly unconnected world. Younger members may find the source of their passion not in the family business but in the family itself.

The stories I use as examples in this book are an intentional co-mingling of my experiences, both personal and professional. I am fortunate to have shared in the journeys of so many remarkable families, including my own. In every situation, I am inspired and encouraged by the resilience, perseverance and selflessness of the families who work together on a shared family vision.

While no path is always perfectly smooth, your path to success doesn't need to be bumpy. Armed with the ideas and approaches outlined in this book, you'll be ready to head into the future, putting your family enterprise—and your family— on the path to continued success.

1

TO SELL OR
NOT TO SELL

L ET'S BE HONEST, the ownership of your business must
change at some point if the business is to continue beyond
your lifetime. But therein lies a challenge. For many business
owners, the answer to the question of whether to sell to non-
family members or transfer ownership to the upcoming generation is not straightforward. The decision rests not only on a
clear financial analysis but also on an often-unclear emotional
analysis. In my work, I've come across three kinds of approaches
to making this decision. I'll call them "Ollie the Ostrich," "Consider and Then Avoid" and "Let's Wrestle This Octopus."

The "Ollie the Ostrich" Approach
The desire to ignore the question of selling or passing ownership to the upcoming generation comes about for many reasons,
four common ones being fear of poverty, fear of conflict, fear of
facing mortality and fear of losing control.

The accountant in me suggests the first of these fears is the
easiest one to address, because it is mostly a quantitative exercise. As a business owner, you may worry that you have not
amassed sufficient financial resources outside of your business

to support your desired lifestyle for the remainder of your life. That makes transferring ownership and/or leadership to the upcoming generation feel like a big risk.

If you have questions about your personal financial position or your long-term lifestyle needs, it can be helpful to consult an independent financial planner—one who isn't incentivized in any way by the firm they work for to sell you something like insurance or investment products—so that they can run projections based on your situation. You can even seek out a couple of financial planners in order to compare the outcomes of their likely differing projections. Keeping in mind that financial projections are estimates, they can paint a picture of your financial future, albeit with broad brush strokes rather than laser precision. The point is, this information can at least give you some idea as to whether or not your fear of poverty is realistic.

As for fear of conflict, fear of facing mortality and fear of losing control, this trio of concerns comes as a package deal. Conflict, or a difference of opinion, is a normal and natural part of life. Whether you sell and reinvent yourself or transfer ownership of your business to the upcoming generation, differences of opinion will surface. The more family members you have, the more differences of opinion there will likely be. However, burying your head in the sand and avoiding the sell-or-transfer question won't eliminate conflict over your decision. It will simply defer the decision until you die. Given that the likelihood of mortality isn't open for debate, letting your fear of conflict prevent you from making a proactive decision about the future ownership of your business ironically means giving up control over one of the most important decisions you will ever have the opportunity to make. It's a decision that impacts not only your legacy but also the personal lives and career choices of your key stakeholders, including family members and key management. So consider embracing and welcoming a lively and engaged discussion—it will be beneficial.

In the worst-case Ollie the Ostrich scenario, ignoring this question and the reality of the future health of your business, a sale can become a forced crisis-management decision. You've suddenly reached a point where you've done all you can do, the financial projections for the business haven't been good for a long time, and the future of the industry hasn't looked favorable for years. Your business needs another cash injection, and your banker, venture capital partner, loan shark, etc., are nowhere to be found. At this point, your options have run out, and your ability to negotiate a decent sales price or a refinancing is non-existent. This is the worst possible time to pull your head out of the sand, because the decision has already been made for you and it's unlikely to be to your financial advantage. So, plan now rather than becoming an Ollie the Ostrich.

The "Consider and Then Avoid" Approach

Most in the Consider and Then Avoid group recognize that change is inevitable and that the question of a change in ownership is central to their business's future potential for success or failure. They indicate as much to those around them. Yet these individuals, often already swamped by the day-to-day operations of their business, soon discover that grappling with this topic will involve time and effort, uncertainty and unknowns, especially at the start. The work might even involve some delicate conversations with family members and key management. Without some understanding at the outset about how to proceed and what to expect, the process of transferring ownership to the upcoming generation can appear to hold more potential for pain than for gain. That makes avoiding pain preferable.

The business owner in the Consider and Then Avoid group is confusing to deal with. It is difficult and nerve-wracking for key stakeholders—such as long-term senior employees, family members active in the business and inactive family members in the upcoming generation—to adjust their personal plans around a business owner's plans that keep changing. Hearing from the business owner one day that they are thinking of selling the business and the next that they plan to transfer ownership to the upcoming generation leaves everyone who will be affected by the final decision frustrated.

Remember that key management and family members are trying to figure out their own career and life plans. If the future ownership of the family business remains unclear, the best and brightest key stakeholders may well leave the business or abandon efforts to prepare themselves for joining it, preferring to align their talents and efforts with a future opportunity they can reasonably depend on. There is no point in key management remaining in place if their future livelihood is in question, or in a talented upcoming-generation family member studying and training to become the future CEO of the family business if it is going to be sold. In these scenarios, the business suffers, since it can be robbed of critical human and intellectual resources, which it relies on for success. A business like this can become fragile, dying a slow death.

The "Let's Wrestle This Octopus" Approach

Octopus Wrestlers tackle the topic of future ownership in an open and transparent way, especially with regard to their key stakeholders. I say, good for them and their spirit of adventure, which is likely the same spirit that can be partially credited for their having created a successful business. While business owners in this group recognize that an answer may not be readily available at the start of the process, keeping key stakeholders informed of the process as it unfolds provides them with some assurance about the stability of the business operations. Octopus Wrestlers understand that working through all the angles and consequences of an outright sale or a transfer to the upcoming generation can strengthen not only the business but also the family as a whole.

WHICHEVER GROUP you fall into, it's essential to be careful when floating the idea of selling your business. Uncertainty about ownership can be damaging not only to your business's relationships with its key stakeholders but also to your business operations. When an owner offhandedly starts talking about selling a business, that business can suddenly begin operating as though there is a big "For Sale" sign on the door. A seemingly casual comment may have a debilitating impact. Catching wind that the owner is fishing for offers can result in key employees beginning job searches elsewhere, suppliers looking for new companies to do business with and clients considering alternative purchasing options to meet their needs. A dynamic business into which everyone associated with it once breathed life and energy can—seemingly without reason—lose its sparkle and zest, descending into operational maintenance, a holding pattern as the owner waits for a buyer to come along.

While there are certainly some strategic reasons for a business owner to fish for offers, this can be done without inflicting damage on the business. For instance, some owners go through a business valuation exercise in order to have a benchmark value for share pricing. One method for determining a value for the business that doesn't rock the boat is to hire a professional business valuator (a good business valuator is well worth the expense), perhaps even on a regular basis—for instance, every three, five or seven years—so that the valuation is seen as part of the normal course of doing business, a way to take the temperature of the business and assess its return on investment. Many business builders and owners discover that a good business valuator is worth their weight in gold.

It's important to keep in mind, however, that there can be a vast difference between what we think something is worth and what someone is willing to pay for it. At the extreme end, I have witnessed sales of private businesses in which the sales price far and away exceeds any traditional means of valuation.

I refer to these as "hit the bid" sale opportunities, where the offer price is so insanely irresistible that a deep analysis of the sell-or-transfer question may not be necessary. These are offers any reasonable business owner must seriously consider, especially when they defy the normal measure of quantitative analysis—for instance, selling for an astronomical price when the business has never even turned a profit. At these kinds of prices, the business owner can afford to be less concerned about the emotional factors tied to a sale—like a loss of sense of purpose, of personal and family identity, or of work as a source of relationships—because they will have significant financial resources to allow them to recreate those factors elsewhere, perhaps in another business or a private charitable foundation.

A word of caution, though: Business owners who sell in these situations can be blindsided by the dislocation the event creates for themselves and their family members. To help people adjust to their new role at the helm of significant liquid financial wealth, as opposed to the illiquid wealth tied up in the private business they used to own, it can be a good idea to create a Family Office. (I'll say more about that in Chapter 9.) For the serial business builder, reinvention can arise after this kind of sale, as the individual recognizes that the business they just sold was only a start for them and that their next step is to build another business. If that's the route a business builder plans to take, it is advisable to consider a number of factors, including the role luck played in the high sales price and whether your business model that led to your previous success is repeatable.

In the real world, thinking strategically about the sell-or-transfer question involves addressing the following factors: the company's long-term business vision and strategy, the purpose of a sale, the alternatives to a sale and the implications of a sale. The long-term business vision and strategy are essential starting points. A long-term vision for a family business needs to be intrinsically inspiring to the upcoming generation, and the strategy needs to indicate the business will be financially robust. In other words, a key requirement for an upcoming generation of engaged owners to be willing to invest their time, efforts and energies in the business is that the business must be financially sustainable. No individual owner will be interested in inspiring visions if they lead to a financially unsustainable business or, worse, to personal financial hardship.

From a long-term point of view, the ability of a privately owned business to be a net cash generator can offset the need for rapid growth of the business. One of the unique characteristics of privately held businesses is that the owners can sacrifice short-term growth for long-term sustainability. Public companies, on the other hand, are mostly driven by the quest for quarterly growth, a sometimes unwise short-term indicator of business vitality. I'm reminded of the fable about the tortoise and the hare, where slow and steady wins the race. If your business is profitable and cash-producing, then slow growth in an industry and a business you know well, along with the ability to be in control of your destiny, can be preferable to being a passive investor in someone else's business.

The reasons for deciding to sell can be numerous and varied. Maybe selling was always your long-term plan and you're now nearing the age where you promised your spouse you would sell, or maybe you're considering selling to meet the immediate financial needs of the business.

There's not much I can say about the spouse scenario, other than reminding you that your decision doesn't affect just you. If your thinking on the issue of selling has changed, now's the time to discuss it. I've witnessed the negative impact on business and family relationships in cases where there have been late-in-life changes to long-held, clearly communicated plans. Managing the expectations of a spouse is as important as managing the expectations of the upcoming generation. If you want to change a previously communicated plan, have a conversation with your spouse in which you explain why you're reluctant to leave your business, and why you want to continue to spend your precious time on the business working in the office with your employees and clients and not traveling the world with your beloved spouse. Ironically, this might be the moment you discover that your spouse is also having second thoughts about you spending more time around the house with them, intruding on their well-established solo lifestyle. You wouldn't be the first to find this out. Either way, have the conversation, be clear about what you both want and come to an understanding before you decide whether or not to sell.

As for selling to meet an immediate financial need in your business, that requires practical financial analysis, including an honest assessment of not only your business's current financial needs but also its projected financial needs. If a financial deficiency is discovered, there may be alternatives to an outright 100% sale of your business. For instance, it might be worthwhile to consider an alternative form of financing, like a partial sale.

Family Offices and wealthy families are a growing source of private family equity investors. These can be more attractive than traditional private equity investors, because the investment goals of Family Offices and wealthy families may better line up with the investment needs of privately owned multigenerational family businesses. Unlike financing via traditional private equity investors, such as angel investors, or venture capital—or, as one family I worked with coined it, "vulture capital"—this kind of financing can be sought to meet the immediate and ongoing liquidity needs of the business. Unlike bank financing, it doesn't weaken the balance sheet, thereby leaving your business open to the possibility of future borrowing if needed. Some private family equity investors may be looking for long-term global partnerships and diversification, while others may be looking for three- to five-year commitments with heavy multiple returns on their initial investment. In the final analysis, if a privately owned business, like yours, becomes a multigenerational family business, it normally has a much longer investment time horizon. This means your business's lifespan will often outlive the terms of a financial relationship with this kind of private family equity investor. Although more prevalent and fashionable today, this financial strategy was key when my brother Arthur and I sought out private family equity investors, brothers John and Bruce McCaw of the US company McCaw Cellular.

If the private family equity investor route is considered, be certain to expand your regular due diligence to investigate, along with their general reputation, these possible partners' knowledge and understanding of your industry, if there is sufficient trust and cultural understanding between your businesses, their knowledge and understanding of the special traits of family businesses, and, of course, their track record as private family equity investors with other family businesses. Private family equity investors may solve your immediate financial needs and, thanks to the added expertise they can offer—knowledge and expertise on topics like family business strategy, professionalizing management, family enterprise frameworks and financial discipline—can provide the bonus of substantially improving your current operations and preparing your private business for long-term success. In my family's case, the McCaw brothers were excellent private family equity investors.

Standing back and thinking strategically about the sell-or-transfer decision also allows you to consider your business beyond its day-to-day operations. There might be ways you could work *on your business* that would easily increase its value, like doing more long-term strategic planning, professionalizing your management or strengthening your decision-making processes. The things you do to improve operational efficiencies might also make your business more profitable, and more financially viable in the long term, giving you an energized sense of purpose and making thoughts about the sale of your business a moot point. It's similar to remodeling the kitchen of your family home to get an improved sales price—only to discover you now love where you live and never want to leave.

Business owners are in the best position to let go when they are financially secure themselves and they know the upcoming generation believes in stewardship of the business for the benefit of all stakeholders, both today and in the future. Upcoming generations are best able to take on the mantle of ownership when they can show they are competent, self-reliant and capable of assuming ownership. Even if the business owner is an Ollie the Ostrich, there usually isn't anything preventing the upcoming generation from organizing themselves.

The upcoming generation will be equipped to handle the potential challenges of a family business transfer when they truly appreciate how difficult and daunting it is for the current family business leader to take their hands off the helm. Younger family members need to recognize that this process of stepping back is typically unknown territory for the current business leaders, often their parents. These leaders aren't perfect and will likely make mistakes not only as they prepare to let go of control but also during and after the handover process. While this is happening, the upcoming generation needs to show that they accept and respect them for doing their best with the information and understandings they have. Further, the members of the upcoming generation will be best able to navigate this uncharted territory when they have already taken responsibility for their own lives, both personally and financially. So get financially secure yourself and encourage financial independence in the upcoming generation.

It seems true that quite often we don't fully appreciate what we have until it's gone, and a privately owned business is a very good example of this. To value this kind of business only on its financial returns is to overlook the other benefits a privately held business can bring to a family: the psychological returns. There is almost always more at stake than money. For family members, the business may offer a sense of pride and belonging, an opportunity to do something together and to give future generations something to connect over. The impact of an outright sale on the daily life of a business leader and owner and family members can therefore be profound. The truth is, the sale of a private business can be a traumatic event, resulting in the loss of connectedness to family and community and the end of younger family members' dreams to one day work in the business.

For these reasons and more, a business owner may choose to transfer the ownership of the business to upcoming family members rather than selling it. However, even if your business has a long-term, energizing vision and a realistic strategy for achieving its long-term goals, turning it into the hub of your family enterprise might be one of the most intimidating decisions you make. In the transition phase from first generation to second generation, it requires being comfortable with ambiguity and being able to handle uncertainty at a very high level. Most of the work in this phase is family-focused and oriented on future generations, so the impact of your decisions might not be measurable until long after you are gone.

However, for those willing to take the leap, the benefits gained in this transition are many, including shared family learning with regard to the management and ownership of a business; strengthened individual and inter-family communication and trust; the pride of shared ownership; an opportunity for social interaction and connectedness with a trusted group of like-minded family members in an increasingly disconnected world; an opportunity to learn and practice leadership skills; and a chance to grow the social capital of the family—the kind of capital that comes about when the bonds of trust and a commitment to the greater good of the family become invaluable psychological assets of a successful multigenerational family enterprise.

The conventional default answer to the question of whether to sell or transfer to an upcoming generation is an outright sale. This may, after full analysis, be the best answer in your situation. However, today more than ever before, if a business is robust, a successful transfer to the upcoming generation and an accompanying continuity plan are within your grasp. The decision requires the kind of thoughtful consideration and honest assessment that great business leaders have already demonstrated as they built a successful business. Being clear that this is work of both the head and the heart, taking a step away from conventional wisdom can change not only your destiny but also the destiny of your business and your family today and for many generations to come.

2

WHY FAMILY BUSINESS TRANSITIONS FAIL

A SUCCESSFUL FAMILY BUSINESS transition is one that results in the continuation of a thriving business after an intergenerational transfer of ownership. Just as building a business does, successful family business ownership transfers require preparation, discipline and an honest, clear-headed sense of the job before you. Research from the early twenty-first century indicates that the failure rate of family business transitions is an astounding 70% in each generation. This means that if ten first-generation families develop transition plans, only one of those families will remain in control of the business by the third generation. Here's how it works:

FIRST-GENERATION TRANSITION:

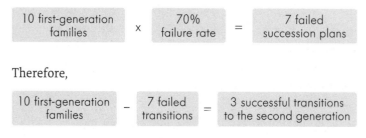

| 10 first-generation families | × | 70% failure rate | = | 7 failed succession plans |

Therefore,

| 10 first-generation families | − | 7 failed transitions | = | 3 successful transitions to the second generation |

SECOND-GENERATION TRANSITION:

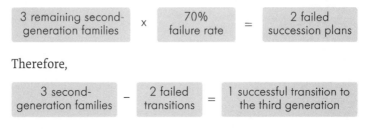

Therefore,

THIRD-GENERATION TRANSITION:

And not only that, as I noted in my first book, *Build Your Family Bank*, this failure rate has remained consistent throughout recorded history, giving rise to the proverb "shirtsleeves to shirtsleeves in three generations." Tellingly, variations of this proverb can be found around the world, translating to such phrasings as "rags to rags," "clogs to clogs," "barn stall to barn stall" and "rice paddy to rice paddy" in three generations. Thus, it appears that transition plans are equally likely to fail, whether they are crafted in countries with the lowest possible tax rates or in those with the highest rates, in old-world cultures or newer ones.

Business scholars, experts and economists have attempted to explain this tenacious failure rate. In their 2003 book *Preparing Heirs: Five Steps to a Successful Transition of Family Wealth and Values*, Roy Williams and Vic Preisser write about how they detected common themes in their many years of estate and financial planning work. By observing business-owning families over multiple generations, they discovered that the traditionally recommended legal and accounting structures for family business transitions were not, on their own, enough to help families avoid the "shirtsleeves to shirtsleeves in three generations" scenario.

Through a joint initiative between their company, The Williams Group, and a global organization called The Executive Committee International (TEC), Williams and Preisser performed specific research in this area, carrying out 3,250 confidential conversations with private business owners at different points in their transition plans. In analyzing the data drawn from these interviews, Williams and Preisser found that "the origins of the 70% failure rate lie within the family itself." They identified four specific causes for this and assigned percentages to indicate how often these causes were cited (summarized as follows):

60%	Breakdown in communication and trust within the family unit
25%	Unprepared heirs
12%	Lack of mission
3%	Failures of professionals

Let's examine these four causes more closely.

Breakdown in Communication and Trust within the Family Unit

Because trust is critical, I'm addressing it before issues around communication. Trust is an essential human experience. It is the most fundamental gel in every human relationship; without it, no relationship can be held together, let alone flourish. When family members feel safe, trust is created. When each family member can fully rely on the others, the family has the potential to achieve something great.

The more time I've spent working with families the more I've come to realize how crucial a role trust plays across the generations in helping family businesses to remain family-controlled and financially robust. My experience has shown me that no effective communication can take place between family members in low- or no-trust environments, where the simplest decisions can become battlegrounds of indecision and/or disagreement. I've also witnessed the opposite. When trust is high, family members find a way to work through tough, uncomfortable and seemingly impossible decisions, discovering there isn't anything they can't resolve. Trust is just that central.

A successful business ownership transfer within a family requires a myriad of decisions. The work involves balancing the needs of not only traditional stakeholders like owners, management, employees, clients and suppliers but also of family members. The process is not about gaining power or being in charge but about making the best possible decisions. When trust exists, family members can respond to situations on the assumption that family decision makers are putting the needs of every individual, and of the family as a whole, ahead of their own. Putting the family first when making decisions will help to both strengthen trust and enable consensus.

The difficult thing about building trust is that the process isn't mechanical; you can follow a checklist and still not achieve it, because often trust acts in illogical ways. For instance, doing everything you say you're going to do makes you reliable, but not necessarily trustworthy. By the same token, many of us have friends or family who aren't always reliable, but we trust them nonetheless.

Within a family, trust comes from a sense of shared values and beliefs. A very long-term shared journey of a united family depends on the family's ability to surround themselves with family members who believe in the same things. In families where people trust one another, members have the confidence to take risks, to experiment and fail, to explore. They know family members will watch each other's backs and will help each other to get up when they fall.

Effective communication skills are also needed to sustain successful relationships, and this is equally true when it comes to the three constituencies in a family enterprise: family members, family business owners and family business management. When it comes to the future of the business, if these three constituencies aren't communicating effectively, there is a tendency to get stuck in what worked well in the past. But change can't be avoided forever. The world changes, industries change, families change and a business in transition is, by definition, changing. Successfully negotiating all of these changes will require strong communication skills between these three constituencies.

Sometimes, a family business becomes the arena for acting out unresolved family issues. Some experts boil the problem down to individual family members not understanding which hat they are wearing when the group is making decisions or when they are speaking. In other words, people may confuse the priorities of the family with those of family business ownership or family business management. While this can certainly be part of the problem, I have yet to see a situation in which the breakdown in communication in a family arises solely because of the inability of family members to understand which hat they are wearing.

In my experience, breakdowns in communication are most commonly caused by family members carrying resentments and/or unresolved problems from the past into the present. These difficulties usually stem from underlying issues that have nothing to do with the family business itself. In one case, two sixty-plus-year-old sisters, still angry with one another over an incident involving a stolen boyfriend when they were teenagers, continue to carry on their dispute in the family business boardroom through comments like "You always get whatever you want!"

A communication breakdown doesn't always present itself in obvious ways like displays of anger, hostility or yelling. In fact, interactions of this kind may not be manifestations of a communication breakdown at all; they may be a family's culturally normal and acceptable way of working through different opinions when making decisions. A better clue that a communication breakdown is in the works is perfectly reasonable family members at a meeting acting perfectly unreasonably in response to the most straightforward decisions. That kind of behavior makes it difficult for any family enterprise to survive.

Unprepared Heirs

Unprepared heirs, or an unprepared upcoming generation, are a significant threat to successful family enterprise transitions. Once there is an upcoming generation of family members, there is a need to foster a culture of stewardship, responsibility and commitment in the three family enterprise systems: the family, family business ownership and family business management. Nurturing the upcoming generation of leaders will help families build an organized, unified and engaged family and family business ownership groups. However, when it comes to family business management, leadership roles, like the CEO, in later generations can be, and often are, filled by non-family members.

One of the unique traits of a family business is that ownership isn't necessarily something the upcoming generation opted into; instead, ownership often arises as a result of legal and accounting structures put in place on the basis of professional advice. Difficulties can surface when family members find themselves drawn into a family dynamic—a business or an industry—which, at best, they have no interest in or, at worst, they are hostile toward. However, when a family enterprise expends energy to strengthen communication and trust within the family; stimulates pride, excitement and interest through its shared values and vision; provides opportunities for participation; and brings clarity to roles and potential opportunities within the business, family members are more likely to become productive, supportive members of the unified family ownership group.

Some family members in positions of authority seek to micromanage, controlling and making decisions for other family members. As when holding a small bird tightly in your hand, though, you need to be careful; too much control can crush the human and intellectual potential in the upcoming generation. The most successful families are those who unlock the brilliance in members of the upcoming generation rather than imposing their own ideas on that generation. While an original owner might get exactly what they want while in control, both the family and the family business lose over the long term when upcoming family members are robbed of the opportunity to learn how to make decisions both by themselves and also collectively within the family enterprise. By suppressing individually earned voices—voices earned through hard work and consistent efforts to be financially and emotionally independent—the family enterprise can also lose its potential to take the family and/or the business somewhere far more successful and rewarding than anything the current family business leader could have imagined.

The most successful families I've worked with have had a leadership group with the kindness and patience to allow members of the upcoming generation to earn their own independent voice, and consequently their self-worth and self-esteem. The leadership group then invites these individuals to bring their passion and earned voices into the business. Equally important is the ability of the upcoming generation to enter the process with openness, honesty and transparency about what they will try to bring to the family enterprise. From either perspective, the groups work together proactively, anticipating challenges along the way.

Some families are concerned that the upcoming generation lacks passion for the business. In addition, the family business leadership may wonder if family members who are not actively involved will have sufficient passion to do what it takes to help the business grow. Businesses either grow or fail, after all, and growth depends on many things, including passion. Ironically, though, it is sometimes the family leadership who have killed this passion, as I have seen, by things like talking negatively about the business around the upcoming generation, forcing family members to participate in the family business or creating a sense of unfairness by providing different opportunities for different family members.

Passion is, without a doubt, a powerful element in the successful accomplishment of goals. But passion during the process of transition doesn't have to begin with a passion for the business. In working with families through the transition process, I've discovered that some family members don't begin with a passion for the business, often because they don't know enough about their current and potential future relationship to the business and their potential roles and responsibilities during and after the transition. Such people do, however, often begin by demonstrating passion for things like family harmony, family connectedness and leaving a legacy that includes the family business for future generations.

Members of successful multigenerational family enterprises soon realize that the passion they bring to the work they do together is also important. Another way to think about the passion factor is to assess how committed the upcoming generation is to a shared journey. Angela Duckworth, a MacArthur Grant recipient, psychologist, researcher and the author of *Grit: The Power of Passion and Perseverance*, makes a compelling case for the key role that grittiness, which she defined in one interview as "the tendency to sustain interest in and effort toward very long-term goals," plays in achieving goals, explaining that factors like IQ, physical appearance, social intelligence and physical health are not strongly correlated with success. She argues that the strongest correlation to success in ongoing endeavors is grit: having the passion and the perseverance to stick with long-term goals, which is exactly what members of a family enterprise working together will need to be successful over many generations.

Duckworth is often asked how to imbue children with a solid work ethic, passion, perseverance and motivation for the long term. She typically answers, "I don't know." However, research by Dr. Carol Dweck appears to suggest that the key lies in individuals having a "growth mindset." The ability to learn isn't fixed and can change according to one's efforts, Dweck found. When children learn about how the brain changes and grows in response to a challenge, they're much more likely to persevere when they fail, because they don't believe failure is a permanent condition. So believing change is possible increases grittiness, and grittiness helps people do better, which eventually leads to more success. Individuals who exhibit grittiness don't let setbacks discourage them; instead, they learn from them and keep striving to reach their goals. For instance, when there is a breakdown in communication and trust within the family unit, family members have the grittiness to work through these tough patches, learning as they go, committed to reaching their shared goal.

Successful families also recognize that failure is normal and healthy. In fact, unified, productive, successful families get that way because of their response to their shared failures. Michael Jordan captured this concept wonderfully in a Nike commercial from the 1990s, saying, "I've missed more than 9,000 shots in my career, I've lost almost 300 games, 26 times I've been trusted to take the game-winning shot and missed. I've failed over and over and over again in my life, and that is why I succeed." That was one person. Imagine the powerful effect on a group when these failures are experienced collectively.

Multigenerational owners of a family business need to recognize that failure isn't the end point. Each failure is a pivot point moving the transition and the family enterprise one step closer to success. When family members learn together from their failures, when they understand that what they are doing isn't happening *to* them but *for* them, it strengthens the bonds of trust, builds strong interfamily relationships and gives the collective family a gift of resilience that will be invaluable over the generations.

Lack of Mission

The importance of a mission or a vision—and more specifically, I would add, a *shared* vision—can't be overstated in the context of a successful family enterprise. A strong, compelling, shared vision will energize a unified, committed ownership base. With a unified ownership base, harmony is achieved, which means a family business is less likely to be torn apart by the seeds of discontent. I compare the work a family does here to a game of tug-of-war. When family members are aligned on the same side of the table, pulling in the same direction, they will win the game. When family members start pulling in opposite directions, they will lose, ending up in the mud. An epic battle in a high-profile family is the stuff of stories of failed family business transitions that gain significant, often embarrassing, media attention.

Failures of Professionals

According to Williams and Preisser, 3% of family business transitions to family members fail because of the work of professionals. This means that the commonly advised corporate structures, which are mostly established to minimize or defer taxes and control the upcoming generation, and/or the existence of professional non-family management result in failed transition plans not because of the structures created by professionals and the existence of non-family management, but in spite of them.

My family of origin is an excellent example. My father began in business working alongside his own father as a chartered accountant (CA) in public practice. My father went on to have a thriving career as a CA until his retirement from the profession at fifty-eight years of age. By all accounts, he was brilliant with numbers and concepts, and thorough and thoughtful in his approach to every aspect of business.

He was also a visionary leader, a man born ahead of his time, a pioneer who focused his entrepreneurial efforts primarily on media and sport organizations at a time when that was uncommon. At the time of his death in 1994, at the age of seventy-eight, he held the controlling interest in the media conglomerate he had built, Western International Communications (WIC), a publicly traded Canadian company. The broadcasting empire included key radio and television stations across Canada and a controlling shareholder interest in Canadian Satellite Communications (Cancom) and Allarcom Pay Television Limited (owners of Super Channel in western Canada), as well as holdings in Family Channel, Studio Post and Transfer, Home Theatre, and Cellular Vision. However, the acquisition that landed my family most firmly in the media's spotlight was my father's 1974 purchase of the controlling interest in the NHL Vancouver Canucks franchise. His remarkable accomplishments as both a business leader and a philanthropic leader were recognized with many awards, including inductions into the Canadian Business Hall of Fame, the Hockey Hall of Fame and the Canadian Association of Broadcasters Hall of Fame.

While I am exceptionally proud of my father, I did not write those last two paragraphs solely to brag about him. The point I wanted to make here is that despite claims to the contrary, both during his lifetime and immediately after his passing, this very successful businessman drew on his professional skill set, which included a deep knowledge of the tax code and of corporate structures, to put in place a comprehensive, technically crafted, legally advised family enterprise structure that allowed for family ownership and professional non-family management after his passing. However, family members relinquished ownership of the robust media empire, in spite of the legal structures and professional management he had put in place.

AS YOU MOVE from privately owning your business toward creating a multigenerational family enterprise, I'd like to pass along something a friend of mine, Chelsea Welch, once said to me: "It's not that the grass is greener on the other side. It's that the grass is greener where you fertilize it." In other words, it's not that other family enterprises are coincidentally successful. It's that the family members in successful family enterprises proactively tackle, through the process of working together, the primary reasons for failure by strengthening trust and communication within the family, preparing the upcoming generation for their potential future roles and responsibilities, and creating a compelling and energizing shared vision. Family enterprises that fertilize the grass in this way have a far greater likelihood of achieving a multigenerational family enterprise that sprawls across acres of luscious, rolling green lawns.

3

FAMILY
ENTERPRISE
BASICS

A FAMILY ENTERPRISE THAT includes an active family
business often finds the business is the engine of the
enterprise, with family members as the engineers. This kind
of situation begins with a passionate entrepreneur who builds
a privately owned business that doesn't just succeed—it flourishes. If the business builder then allows ownership to transfer
to the upcoming generation, they may be putting the business
on the track to become the financial core of a multigenerational
family enterprise.

As noted earlier, there are various approaches the business
builder can take to this transfer of ownership. Some owners avoid discussing transition plans with the upcoming generation, possibly because they want to avoid creating conflict
among siblings or simply because they don't know where to
begin. Instead, the success or failure of the transition is left
to fate. In some cases, fate can be kind. If the upcoming generation comprises siblings, a small number of people who have
grown up together with the business at the core of the family
and have strong relational bonds with each other and with the
business, this generation has a good chance of having a high

level of trust, workable communication skills, shared values and the ability to develop a shared vision. If there are also some strong business skills in this sibling group, the business may continue to thrive.

However, the cousin group is a different story. This is usually a larger number of people who have not grown up together, often not even in the same town, or around the business and do not necessarily feel emotionally connected to the family business. This group does not share the same parents and may not have intense relationships across the extended family. It will take more than chance to build trust, effective communication skills and commitment to shared values and vision among this broad group of individuals.

So, how do you increase your chances of a successful ownership transfer? By understanding the basics of successful multigenerational family business transitions. The primary differences between the operations of a family business and a business controlled by a more diverse group of shareholders relate to the family factor and the unique systems at work in a family enterprise.

There are three fundamental systems in a family enterprise, each with a different set of responsibilities:

a) THE FAMILY: Responsible for the articulation of shared values and the development of a shared vision for the *family's* human, intellectual and financial assets.

b) FAMILY BUSINESS OWNERSHIP: Responsible for the articulation of shared values and the development of a shared vision and/or goals for the family business, in conjunction with the family's shared values and vision. Family business ownership is also responsible for ensuring that family business management is effectively working to meet these objectives.

c) FAMILY BUSINESS MANAGEMENT: Responsible for developing a strategic plan that shows how the family business owner-ship's shared values, vision and goals for the business will be achieved.

With regard to the family factor, a family business has a unique group of shareholders: multiple generations of family members whose connection to the business often arises involuntarily through birth or marriage. A successful family business must find a way to work with this group of shareholders. The most effective way to do it is to proactively engage the group as participants in the family enterprise, and that means educating them on family enterprise basics such as Earning a Voice, Family Meetings, Ownership and Leadership.

Earning a Voice

It always amazes me when family members believe they are entitled to a voice in family enterprise decisions simply by virtue of birth or marriage. Birth or marriage can give family members a seat at the family table and a voice in *discussions* about the family's shared values and vision. Beyond those conversations, however, consider the advantages to be gained when family members are expected to earn a voice before having input into *decisions* that require a level of expertise, like decisions on the future direction of the family business, mergers and acquisitions, investments, employment, compensation, etc. When everyone knows that decisions are being made by respected family members who are qualified to make them, trust in the decision-making process is increased, along with acceptance and support for the decisions themselves. Regretta-bly, my experience with families has shown me that the oppo-site is also true. When a jumble of family members who don't trust or respect one another and are qualified only through birth or marriage to have a voice are involved in the decision-making process, there is a lack of confidence in and support for either the process or the decisions that are made.

Your family enterprise is strengthened when you agree not to allow unearned voices at the decision-making table. Making this official early—early being a very important point—in the generational transition process can eliminate many problems, including family members who would rather focus on demands for dividends or personal liquidity than on the stewarding of the financial health of the family enterprise, including the family business, for current and future generations. Allowing a family member who has not earned a voice—and worse, is unqualified and inexperienced—to weigh in on things like cash management in the family business, or a parent who is not active in the family business to weigh in on their child's salary, can easily lead to weak decision-making and potentially disruptive conflict. While this may seem obvious once it's pointed out, it's often not considered beforehand.

Each family will develop its own list of criteria for earning a voice within each of the three systems in the family enterprise. Those criteria will reflect the unique nature of your family and your family business. At the family level, the basic qualities many families look for, however, include being able to disagree without becoming emotional; putting the needs of the whole family first; being the kind of person other family members can respect, by demonstrating a good work ethic, dedication and expertise in one's vocation; being trustworthy; extending trust to fellow family members; being willing to admit when one is wrong; and demonstrating the ability to be financially independent of the family. This last point is important, since individuals who are able to stand on their own two feet are better equipped to put the long-term needs of the collective family ahead of their personal or individual family branch's financial needs.

When family members are clear about what it takes to earn a voice in any of the three family enterprise systems—the family, family business ownership and family business management—expectations are easily managed, and each member can choose to do what is needed to earn a voice in the decision-making process. In the end, no matter how you and your family define an earned voice, all earned voices should be welcomed and encouraged.

Family Meetings

Family meetings are essential in any family enterprise. Successful multigenerational families know that working together in harmony to make good decisions greatly increases the likelihood of achieving long-term goals. Individuals are not always born with the natural ability to collaborate with others, even those to whom they are closely related. However, this is a skill set that can be learned, and like any skill, the more it is practiced the stronger it will become. Family meetings give family members a place to learn how to work together. Each time a family has a successful meeting, in which members not only share their own perspectives but also listen to the ideas of others, the group's collaboration skills are strengthened. And by strengthening their ability to work well together, families can prepare themselves to collectively handle the unforeseen challenges that arise on any multigenerational journey.

Additionally, family meetings are the most effective forum for averting the primary causes of failed family business transitions. As members participate in creating the family's shared future through family meetings, these meetings become a place to strengthen trust and communication, to prepare the upcoming generation for their future roles and responsibilities, and to reinforce shared values and develop a shared vision. Family meetings are also an effective way to provide clarity and transparency about the decisions made by the family enterprise, thereby strengthening unity and commitment to the decisions made in the pursuit of the family's long-term goals.

In case holding a family meeting is something you're not yet comfortable with, allow me to walk you through the process. Keeping in mind that you already have a full life, as do your family members, in most cases family meetings only need to be held twice a year at most. Unless a traumatic event has occurred within the family or the business, such as the sudden death of a family leader or the crashing of the industry in which the business operates, more than two family meetings a year, especially in the formative years, can exhaust family members and make them apprehensive about the process. On top of having already full personal and professional lives, some family members may also have to travel great distances or give up weekend or vacation time to attend. Additionally, productive family meetings involve a lot of learning. The time in between meetings gives everyone the opportunity to digest what they have learned and to prepare for the next meeting.

Determination, persistence and commitment are good character traits for everyone to bring to the family enterprise and the family business. However, even with all these traits in place, 100% attendance at every meeting is likely not achievable, but do consider ways to ensure the highest attendance rate possible. Some families set annual dates—the first Saturday in May and November, for instance—to allow family members to schedule the meeting well in advance, which increases the likelihood of attendance. To encourage younger family members, who may be more focused on their own lives, to attend, consider strategies such as assigning them responsibility for an item on the agenda, holding meetings later in the day or finding ways to build more fun into the meetings.

The next thing to consider is who to invite. My experience indicates that everyone above a certain age, say sixteen, can be invited to the first few meetings, because these usually focus on exploring the levels of trust and strength of communication in the family through discussing what should be a non-contentious topic: the family's shared values. If difficulties emerge at this stage, I encourage the family leadership to seek additional expertise from a family meeting facilitator, a family enterprise advisor or a conflict resolution coach.

A well-run family meeting is planned well in advance. It has an agenda that outlines the topics to be discussed, with responsibility assigned to someone for each topic and suggested allocations of time. This agenda should be circulated well in advance of the meeting, to allow invitees to offer input. Soon after the meeting is held, detailed minutes should be circulated in draft form to all those who attended. Once any needed revisions, additions and/or deletions have been made, a final version of the minutes should be sent to all of the meeting invitees, whether or not they were in attendance.

These minutes form the recorded history, including both ups and downs, of the family's commitment to building a successful relationship between the family and the family business. They also promote accountability and transparency. Accountability is created when the minutes record who in the family is responsible for what. And when family members follow through on their recorded commitments, the family's trust in those individuals is strengthened. Minutes provide transparency by documenting the decisions that were made and the policies that were created. By including a summary of the discussion, including the voting results, the minutes capture decisions that weren't unanimous but still gained the full support of the family. Further, recording the process gives upcoming generations a starting point for future decisions.

Since they are written in the knowledge that they will form part of the historical record for upcoming generations, family meeting minutes should capture meaningful conversations and decisions but be scrubbed of the delicate interactions that will likely occur at times among family members.

Shared learning is an important element in family meetings, and it's a good way to encourage participation and prepare younger family members on a variety of topics. Keep in mind that the goal of family shared learning is "good enough": not perfect, because perfect isn't possible. Overall, when you set out on a shared learning program, clarify your objectives, get input from family members and pace yourselves. In other words, shared learning should encourage involvement of family members. Shared learning topics will be different for every family enterprise, because they will reflect the priorities, needs and interests of both individual family members and the business. Some advisors refer to this as the education component of family meetings, but to me that sounds too much like a teacher-student relationship. In the shared learning components I have led, family members aren't students in the classroom. They are adults learning together, gaining knowledge and sharing thoughts and ideas.

Some writers on the subject of family meetings encourage the inclusion of spouses. My personal experience has been different, especially with regard to initial family meetings. The intention of those meetings is not to exclude spouses but to focus first on building trust, communication and team-building skills among the individuals who will one day be in the legal ownership/shareholder position of making decisions together. Once all the team members are comfortable working together, then spouses are invited to join (which they may opt not to do, of course). In strengthening the bonds of trust and communication, the work is best done like the ripples that spread out when a stone is dropped in a still pond, starting with the smallest generational group possible and then expanding out, one additional group of family members at a time. In the meantime, in order to strengthen trust by providing clarity and transparency, spouses can have access to the detailed minutes from the meetings.

Ownership

The topic of ownership is a good one for shared learning in family meetings. Ownership is an area of family business basics where things get really interesting, because after the first generation of business builders, where ownership is voluntary, ownership in the upcoming generation is quite often involuntary. In fact, it's common for the upcoming generation to become business owners at a young age as a result of complex legal and accounting work to defer or minimize taxes. This involuntary ownership can have a cascading impact on the family, individual family members and the family business.

Confusion, frustration and tension can arise between these two kinds of owners. What might look like a pot of gold to the business builder and voluntary owner can feel more like a golden burden to the involuntary owner. The business builder might expect the upcoming generation to be excited about and grateful for the gift of ownership. Yet the upcoming generation might be uncomfortable about taking on the role of owner, perhaps feeling guilty or like cheaters or imposters. Younger members may even feel overwhelmed by or fearful of the mantle of ownership, after seeing how it has consumed the life of the business builder.

Quite often, when they are young, the only connection the upcoming generation has to their ownership is their signature on the last page of the annual tax return for some legal entity of the family enterprise. It's usually best to have ownership conversations in an age-appropriate way, focusing on what you want for the upcoming generation. For instance, if your goal is for younger family members to lead purposeful, financially independent lives, I'd suggest asking yourself if providing detailed corporate financial information could potentially derail them from this pursuit. Financially unsophisticated family members may not understand that the assets of the family business are not the same as the assets of the family.

There is a journey the upcoming generation travels between youth and successfully stepping into their potential adult roles as owners and stewards of the family business. Once they are old enough to do so, you may want to encourage family members to read the documents they are signing—and you'd be surprised at just how many people do not read documents before signing them. (You might be less surprised to hear that many difficulties that arise in later years can be directly traced back to this practice of signing without reading.) You can also ask a trusted individual like a family leader or a professional to explain in an age-appropriate way what the documents are about. This is a good time as well for family leaders to talk about the purpose of the business and the role of the family factor, what the business stands for and the role stewardship will play. That will be much more effective than an offhanded comment like "One day all this will be yours."

As the upcoming generation matures, so should the discussion around money matters. For adult children, reviewing financial documents provides an opportunity to build the financial acumen that they will need as the upcoming generation of owners. This is a good time to continue the conversation not only about the purpose of money in the family but also its role in the business. The details can be complicated for non-accountants, but that doesn't mean the conversation shouldn't happen. In fact, if a family has a complex legal family enterprise structure, the purpose of money is a topic that shouldn't be avoided, because the chance of misunderstanding the need for cash flow between entities is high.

In many instances, I've found that upcoming family members will go on for decades signing the last page of tax returns and legal documents they know nothing about, other than that the paperwork is "the trust tax return" or "it has something to do with the family's holding company." What begins in youth as an unquestioning action based on the request of a family leader, often a parent, can develop into an adulthood habit of not wanting to question the details of these often complex documents, resulting in missed learning opportunities and unadvisable conditioning. And when adult family members discover they have questions and no answers, they are likely to fill the gaps in their knowledge with their own erroneous assumptions. For instance, four siblings in the upcoming generation may have been signing corporate tax returns, discovering they are each 25% shareholders. Then, noticing the final taxable amount, they could make the assumption that if they could just find a way to get their hands on it, 25% of that money would be theirs. They aren't aware that the family business has specific needs for that cash, which could include things like financing debt or business growth, or funding a war chest for shareholder redemptions or operations if there is an economic downturn that affects the business. Timely conversations not only clear up misunderstandings but are also a good way to educate the upcoming generation of owners about a vital topic: the role of cash and cash management in any business.

Another belief common among members of the upcoming generation is that the owner is also the one running, operating or managing the business. And a first-generation builder typically *is* the one running, operating or managing the business, making the operating owner the most familiar form of ownership to the upcoming generation. That often creates a lack of understanding about the job or the role of ownership in a family business.

A shared learning component in family meetings can open up the discussion, explaining to everyone that there are other kinds of owners, aside from the operating owner, involved in day-to-day operations. The range of ownership masterfully captured on pages 11–12 of one of Craig E. Aronoff, Stephen L. McClure and John L. Ward's books, *Family Business Ownership: How to Be an Effective Shareholder*, includes:

· GOVERNING OWNER: A full-time overseer but not involved in operations; sometimes referred to as the Chair of the Board.

· ACTIVE OWNER: Not employed in the business but takes a genuine interest and is attentive to all the business's issues.

· PROUD OWNER: Not knowledgeable about the business or engaged in it, but still proud to be an owner.

· PASSIVE OWNER: Merely collects dividends, making no conscious decision to stay an owner; is often stuck and therefore along for the ride.

· INVESTOR OWNER: Like a passive owner, but if satisfied with returns, makes a conscious decision to remain an owner, similar to investing in the stock markets.

As you consider ownership through this lens, it becomes clear that when a business is in its initial stages, family members might well be managing owners. However, as family members grow in number, interests and capacities and disperse over geographic locations, the likelihood of the family business being able to provide a management job for every family member diminishes to the point where there may be no family members working in the business at all.

Through conversations held on an age-appropriate basis, the upcoming generation will learn that ownership isn't static. Because of tax planning, many younger family members spend years as passive owners. Then, as an example, let's say in early adulthood a member of the upcoming generation becomes an active owner but also enters an intense internship program for a period of time to complete their medical doctor degree, at which point they might shift from being an active owner to a proud owner. Once the internship ends and they have more time, this family member might shift back to being an active owner. Over a lifetime, it is natural for a family member's level of ownership involvement to change from time to time.

Ownership is key to the survival of any business, and a family business is no different. While all family members can be active owners at the same time, not all can be proud or passive owners at the same time. Ownership sets the values, vision and mission of the business, while management creates the strategic plan to achieve that vision and mission. At least one person associated with the family ownership group, even if it's a trusted representative from the advisory board in times of need, must always be at the helm as an active owner. Without that, management's accountability to the strategic plan, which is the articulation of the ownership's shared values and vision, can disappear, setting adrift a once well-charted family business.

Family business owners require the same fundamental knowledge that any kind of business owner needs. The topics that could be addressed through shared learning in family meetings include:

- The ability to read and understand financial statements.
- The basics of the family business and the industry it's involved in.
- The culture of the family business and how owners contribute to that culture.
- The concept of strategy as it relates to your family business.
- Cash management; trade-offs between ownership liquidity, dividends and family business reinvestment.
- The role of owners' work, independent of family.

· The challenges of placing trust in management.
· The principles of family business decision-making.
· Owners' legal rights and responsibilities.
· Employment and compensation in the family business.

The strategic plan clarifies the specific goals of the family business, indicates how those goals are realistic and creates a detailed roadmap as to how the goals will be achieved. For that reason, the strategic planning process is something in which the owners, or representatives from the ownership group, should be involved. The process encourages open communication between ownership and management, aligns owners' shared values and vision with the family business, and provides ownership with a blueprint to assist with decision-making that affects the agreed-upon strategic plan.

Having open conversations about the ownership structure, both today and in the future, will help prepare the upcoming generation to take the helm. Further, this kind of transparency builds emotional ownership by the family—one of the things that sets a family business apart—and demonstrates trust in the upcoming generation. Though they may seem difficult in the beginning, these conversations are one of the most important investments you can make for the successful multigenerational transition of your family business.

Leadership

When I think about leadership, my mind goes to the business section of the bookstore, and its autobiographies by almost mythical leaders like Steve Jobs of Apple and Jack Welsh, who ruled General Electric from 1981 to 2001, and books by learned researchers and inspired speakers like Seth Godin and Simon Sinek. I hope you're not expecting something similar here. What you'll find in this section is an explanation of the often-overlooked leadership roles unique to a family enterprise and some thoughts on successful leadership in a family enterprise.

The number of leadership roles will be different for each family business, based on the talents of the family members and the needs of its three systems (the family, family business ownership and family business management). But whether the titles are Family Leader, Chair of the Board and/or CEO, and whether these positions are filled by the same person or by different individuals, when family is involved, even the most practical issues these leaders have to deal with can become emotional.

In early generations, the family business builder and leader often fills the role of owner, management and family leader. In later generations, some family members will ascend to family business leadership roles through their work and ambitions; others may evolve into a family leadership role they hadn't contemplated as they were growing up.

A *family business leader* is someone who has aspired to and earned the leadership role. It's that person's name at the top of your family business organizational chart. They're the individual ultimately accountable for the success or failure of the business, and they play an integral role in successful family business transition plans. From a business perspective, this is the person who has likely charted a life course to earn their role as leader of the family business ownership and/or management group, gaining leadership skills inside and/or outside the family business, reading books written by the greats, pursuing an applicable education like a professional business degree, joining a peer-to-peer leadership organization, working with a mentor or a coach, etc.

The *family leader,* on the other hand, is the glue in a united family. Unity is something a multigenerational family can't have too much of. And yet the importance of a family leader is often overlooked, not recognized until the family begins to rupture at its weakest points when the current family leader is gone. Family members follow a family leader not because of coercion but out of respect and loyalty for everything the family leader has done to support individual family members and the family as a whole.

No one is born to leadership, and this is just as true for family leaders. One of the challenges for the family leader is that those in later generations may not automatically follow the leader as the second generation (children) often does of the first generation (parents). Children follow parents first out of a need for security and safety and later, for some, as a result of a lifetime habit. In later generations, a family leader is less likely to enjoy such unquestioning acceptance. Members of a larger, more diverse cousin group may question and challenge decisions being made—and this is actually good news. The family enterprise is strengthened when the upcoming generation is curious and open-minded and questions the status quo. A good family leader will encourage this questioning from those who have earned a voice, understanding that differing talents and expertise will be the building blocks for the success of their multigenerational family enterprise.

The upcoming family leader will have to earn followers, and this typically comes about by earning their respect, just as it does for the family business leader. The skill set of a family business leader is fairly easy to assess, perhaps by reviewing their past business successes, their education, and any awards and acknowledgments they have received. The skills of the family leader, on the other hand, are harder to evaluate, but by gaining the family members' trust, the family leader can earn their respect. Without trust, family members will not follow the family leader.

The role of the family leader is a thoughtful and sometimes emotional one, something not entered into lightly—in fact, many family leaders discover doing the right thing is not always the easy thing. Being an effective family leader means putting the needs of the entire family, as well as of individual family members, before their own. It means nurturing the development of each family member while maintaining a focus on the collective good. It means showing you have everyone's back by ensuring accountability to whatever the family's collective goal might be. It means having tough conversations with individuals who threaten the good of the collective family, not to punish them but to help them to get back on course.

Successful family leaders have the empathy and wisdom to understand that family members are a work in progress. This leadership role is often filled by someone a little older, with a few more years of life experience under their belt, because time, and certainly if they've been parents themselves, has a way of making it clear that to be human is to be less than perfect. Family members will slip up and make mistakes, but the family leader is there to give them a soft landing from which to learn from their mistakes. These opportunities to learn further strengthen the bonds of trust within the family.

I read somewhere that one way a family can identify their family leader is that they are the family member who says, "My house, 6:00 p.m. Sunday for dinner," and everyone shows up. However, I've also seen instances where, when it's a parent filling the role, family unity is achieved only because that parent acts as the middleman, the smoother, not having the tough conversations, not holding family members accountable when they slip up, not allowing family members to truly learn from their mistakes. I've attended family meetings after this kind of family leader has died and witnessed the family painfully fall apart, with high levels of distrust and resentment because of unaccountable family members, resulting in feuding destroying their family business. Family leaders must ensure they don't fall into the trap of being middlemen.

Some family members display envy toward family business leaders and family leaders, thinking these leaders have hit the jackpot. In worst-case scenarios, such family members may actively work to block leadership efforts. When this stance is taken, it threatens the family as a whole. To those family members, I would say there is much more to gain by working with someone than against them, especially someone who is working in your personal and the collective family's best interests.

I recommend that leadership blockers think about the added pressure, responsibility and stress a leadership role in a multigenerational family puts on the leader. Leaders are not only accountable to current family members; they are also guardians of the generations of family members who have gone before them and protectors of the generations yet to come. Leaders in family enterprises have a seven-generation mindset, selflessly fulfilling a role even though they will never bear full witness to its successes because in seven generations the current family leader(s) will have long left this earthly plane, giving new meaning to the phrase "delayed gratification."

And then there is non-family leadership, specifically the deciding to professionalize leadership when the family realizes there are no family members in the upcoming generation ready or able to assume leadership of the family business, say as a CEO. The best practices I've seen here involve the family addressing this need as early as possible, not waiting until days before the incumbent family business leader is due to walk out the door into retirement. In fact, in a perfect world, the family business considers the CEO role a priority, planning for the next CEO as soon as a new one is appointed. Some families hire a bridging CEO, someone to fill the role until a longer-term fit can be found externally or family members from the upcoming generation are ready to step in. The best bridging CEOs are individuals who are interested in a ten-year run at most, are in their late fifties or early sixties, have CEO skills, are experienced business leaders and are able to manage the nuanced relationships between family members and the business.

Family enterprises are special entities. To run them successfully requires paying attention to the three fundamental systems at work: the family, family business ownership and family business management. Management is the system that is most easily addressed, since it is taught in business schools across the globe. Less attention has been devoted to ownership, but that system too can be easily handled once the critical role of ownership is understood. The family factor is more challenging because emotions can get in the way of making good decisions. However, by having family enterprise leaders who ensure that family members at the table have earned a qualified voice and schedule regular family meetings to manage the expectations of the upcoming generation, educate the upcoming generation and provide a forum to deal with family issues outside of the family business, the family factor can also be effectively managed. Success can be achieved.

4

TRUST
AND
COMMUNICATION

TRYING TO BUILD A SUCCESSFUL multigenerational family enterprise without trust and strong communication skills among family members is like trying to build a house on quicksand. The good news is that achieving improvement in these areas can be as straightforward as having the willingness to learn, implement and practice these skills.

I always allocate time at the first family meeting I'm facilitating to deliver a shared learning piece on strengthening communication. Some family members may already be apprehensive about the meeting, fearing the frustration that miscommunication has triggered in the past. Addressing the topic of strengthening communication at the start reduces the likelihood of this fear being realized and increases the chances of a smooth meeting with effective communication among family members. And then each smooth meeting thereafter further increases the likelihood of family members willingly attending the next. Over time, family members' practicing strong communication skills in meetings helps to build trust within the family group.

The response I get from families after my presentation is usually something like, "Wow! Why didn't we learn that in school?" to which I respond, "I know! I wish I'd learned this sooner too!" And there is my point. It is very rare for someone to be born a perfect communicator, but fortunately, communication skills can be learned. In this chapter I'll offer some insights I've gained through experience about building trust and strengthening communication.

Trust

I can't overemphasize the importance of trust among family members if they are to work successfully together, especially when the plans are long-term. However, I didn't fully appreciate the impact low trust can have until I worked with a family who, when I first met them, were characterized by simmering anger, frustration and resentment. Every word spoken was misinterpreted, challenged or seen as an opportunity to battle. This family had reached the point where they were spending more time and energy fighting one another than paying attention to the family enterprise.

Luckily, things didn't end there for them. Recognizing that they wanted to succeed multigenerationally and that the path they were on was pulling the family apart, they did find a way to work together. They began by accepting that trust isn't a fixed resource in a family. Trust does not operate in an on/off mode; it is continually being built up or depleted. As they worked to figure out why they had such low levels of trust with one another, the family members discovered that the lack of trust was rooted in issues from the past. Stories from decades prior had been carried forward, imprinting on the individual branches of the family. Because these siblings and cousins were committed to their collective family enterprise, they did the hard work of addressing these stories and, in some cases, letting them go. By putting the needs of the entire family ahead of individual needs, this family took a significant step toward building trust.

As this family continued to work on building trust, I shared with them some takeaways from General Stanley McChrystal on the importance of trust in a team. General McChrystal successfully took charge in 2003 of the US Joint Special Operations Command, which led an interservice team that included Army Rangers, Navy SEALs and Delta Force. From the general's work, this family learned that trust is a key element in high-functioning teams and that building it includes interaction, a chance for team members not only to listen to what people say but also to see their actions up close. Trust is there when people know everyone has each other's backs. In family terms, this means family members who are prepared to work at building strong relationships, who won't give up when times get tough, who will stick with pursuing what they want to achieve and not quit, and who are clear on what they want to achieve collectively and will do their best to get the job done. Building trust includes not only big gestures like putting the needs of other family members or the collective family first, but also smaller ones like verbally expressing trust in someone in front of other people.

This family had a compelling mission and vision for the shared future of the family enterprise. To achieve it, they were willing to work actively to create trust and to pay close attention to anything that might deplete the trust bank they were building up. By starting with the basics—honoring their commitments to one another and to the family as a whole; keeping private family matters private; remaining open, honest, kind and transparent; and making sure family members were informed in a timely fashion if plans changed—they steadily strengthened the bonds of trust among themselves.

This family learned first-hand that building trust takes time and practice. They had slip-ups, but they discovered that pointing fingers didn't build trust; that kind of behavior only reinforced position-taking and a defensive response. Instead, they learned to be patient and kind when mistakes happened, especially during stressful times. Through a commitment to their shared vision, they found the grit to stick with their goal of building trust. Role-modeling this grittiness also paid dividends, as the upcoming generation saw not only that trust can be built up but also how to do it.

Communication

Have you ever had a conversation with someone that didn't go the way you expected, leaving you thinking, "Gee, I wonder what went wrong there"? This next section sheds light on ways in which a conversation may have unintentionally gone wrong.

INTENT, ACTION, EFFECT

Understanding the cycle of communication—which includes intent, action and effect—can be very useful, because a great deal of miscommunication and potential conflict arises during the process. It might interest you to know that every conversation we enter into stands a two-thirds chance of being misunderstood. When we are communicating, only one-third of our communication process, the action part, is public: the words we speak or write, the gestures we make. The other two-thirds, our intent as the communicator and the effect our communication has on the listener and the listener's assumptions, is private. In other words, in two-thirds of communication, you don't know the thinking behind what the speaker is saying and the speaker can't read the listener's mind, including knowing the assumptions the listener is making about the speaker's intentions.

For instance, let's say you are the family member responsible for drafting and circulating minutes after each family meeting. One senior family member always reminds you to get this job done on a timely basis. Let's take a look at this senior family member's possible intent, what they might be thinking:

"Hey, I know how easy it would've been for me to forget something like this at your age. Maybe a little reminder from me will help." That doesn't sound so bad, right? But what if the senior family member communicates this with a snappy comment like "Don't forget to get the minutes out ASAP." Yikes! The effect on you could be something like an irritated and defensive "Does he think I'm useless? I always get the minutes out fast!"

Do you see where I'm going here? The effect our communication has does not necessarily line up with our intentions. Communication easily breaks down when we, as listeners, start by assuming the intention behind someone's words is negative. However, when, as speakers, we pay attention to the effects of our communication and when, as listeners, we assume positive intentions, we increase the likelihood of having positive, dynamic conversations.

Trust plays a significant role in strong, effective, productive communication. When we trust the people we are communicating with, we are more likely to make positive assumptions about their intentions. When trust is low, as it was in the family I described earlier, listeners are more likely to make mainly negative assumptions about the speaker's intentions. Once the family in the example committed to assuming positive intentions, there was a positive shift in their communications with one another. You could almost feel the earth move. One family member took the lead in this regard, displaying commitment to the task of building trust within the family even when their efforts at making positive assumptions weren't initially reciprocated. Eventually, thanks to this family member staying honest, open and genuinely committed to the goal of building trust, the other family members came around.

This family agreed to let go of the small stuff as they worked to reach their larger shared vision. When an issue was particularly troubling, they proceeded by gently and carefully checking in, during facilitated family meetings in some instances, on the speaker's intentions. It wasn't easy to start with, but the family learned a new way to communicate that simultaneously strengthened trust and changed old communication habits that hadn't been working well for them.

GETTING THE MESSAGE ACROSS

Here's an interesting bit of research from Professor Albert Mehrabian, who pioneered the understanding of communication and currently devotes his time to research, writing and consulting as Professor Emeritus of Psychology, UCLA. In his book *Silent Messages: Implicit Communication of Emotions and Attitudes*, his research findings show the percentage of our communication about feelings and attitudes that are understood by others through our various forms of communication. These are:

- NON-VERBAL: Face-to-face—55% (body language, facial expressions, postures, gestures, etc.).

  As an example, you ask your partner, "Are you okay?" With slumped shoulders, moist eyes and a sniffle, your partner responds, "I'm fine." Where is the real meaning in this response—in the body language or in the words they spoke?

- PARAVERBAL: Phone calls—38% (tone, emphasis, the pitch and pacing of our voices).

  As an example, look at what happens to this sentence when the same words are spoken with a different tone, emphasis, pitch and pacing. From the example above, consider a telephone response of a shrill curt "I'm FINE!" or a drawn-out, softly spoken, shaky "I'm . . . fine . . ." or an easygoing singsong tone of "I'm fine." The paraverbal aspect of words strongly influences the message they communicate.

· VERBAL: Email—7% (written words alone).

The written word is very easy to misinterpret. And imagine, the research I've cited here was done before the existence of texting. Think about the chance of miscommunication of our feelings or attitudes when our messages are distilled into so few words. Maybe it's my generation, but I believe texting is a method of communication best left to non-emotional items like confirmation of a meeting time or location.

When it comes to the written word, I have a general piece of advice for families. As a rule, when communicating by email, do not put the recipient's address in the message you are drafting until you have reread your message and are absolutely ready to press "Send." Unlike working with snail mail, which requires finding an envelope for the letter you've handwritten or printed out on paper, a stamp and a trip to the mailbox—many steps that used to give us a moment to pause and consider what we had written—email can go from a momentary thought to publication with the tap of a computer key. You might even consider making it a personal habit not to send anything negative in writing. Bad feelings can be fleeting, but writing them down has a way of making them permanent.

I completely understand that for some families and individuals, the only practical way to communicate with others is via email. It also makes sense at times to get things in writing for the benefit of all. In emotive situations, however, my recommendation is to wait until negative emotions like anger or frustration have subsided. You will then be better able to separate the issue from your feelings and assess what you want your words to achieve and how you can phrase things in a way that won't escalate the issue.

Finally, it's important to recognize the effect that various forms of communication have on trust. Firing off texts and short emails can work well when trust is high and everyone assumes that everyone has the best of intentions. However, when trust is low or a particularly thorny issue needs to be resolved, it's best to meet in a face-to-face environment where there is less chance of miscommunication. Furthermore, showing up in person and demonstrating a genuine commitment to working together to resolve tricky issues gives family members an opportunity to build trust.

USING EFFECTIVE LANGUAGE

When I was studying conflict resolution at the Justice Institute of British Columbia (JIBC), a lot of time was dedicated to building our communication toolboxes. This included learning that sometimes the language we use gets in the way of effective communication. For instance, "why" questions can have a significant impact on effective communication. Asking "why" when you're trying to understand a problem can automatically put your counterpart in a defensive mode. In low-trust or conflict situations, when we hear the word "why," we try to justify our behavior. It's automatic and natural; our brain looks for the quickest way to avoid pain! So, we defend, defend, defend.

When we ask "why," we are generally looking for the root cause of the problem, rather than justification for a behavior or action. And we are not looking for the cause just to know it; we are curious because we want to know how to avoid the same situation in the future. Substituting "why's" with questions along the lines of "What can we do to avoid the problem in the future?", "How can we approach this differently?" or "What can we do to understand the problem?" will do a better job of getting to the root of the issue.

Another communication trait to avoid is the overuse of absolutes like "never" and "always." Absolutes leave no room for a person or situation to change, and their overuse by a family member can eventually cause others to stop listening, which makes problem-solving difficult, if not impossible.

Many of the words we use are automatic and we may not realize something we've said is a problem until someone points it out to us. One of the words I recently became cautious about using is "should," because I have seen its ability to deplete trust. Telling a family member that they should or shouldn't do something can be read as a way of telling them you do not trust them to make good decisions by themselves. "Should" implies judgment, and usually negative judgment at that. Linda Dobson Sayer, a communications specialist and a Certified Conflict Resolution Coach from the JIBC Centre for Conflict Resolution, shared a simple saying with me: "You shouldn't should on other people." I took those words to heart and now use them as guidelines.

And finally, keep an eye on how you use the words "and" and "but." "But" can indicate we are listening with judgment rather than with respect and curiosity. "But" is a default word, a killer of ideas and possibility. On the other hand, "and" expands ideas, which increases possibility—ingredients a successful multigenerational family and family business need in abundance. As a fun exercise, try replacing "but" with "and" in your conversations for a few days. Although it will likely feel awkward at first, you might notice a switch in your attitude toward the ideas being expressed and also a change in the speaker, who will now feel their ideas are being considered as valuable rather than disposable.

TRIANGULATION

If you're a parent, has this ever happened to you? Sibling One has a problem with Sibling Two, and rather than One talking to Two, One comes to you, as the parent, to talk *about* Two. (Or maybe you remember being Sibling One or Sibling Two yourself in your youth.) This situation is common, often starting in a child's formative years as they turn to their parents for advice when learning how to resolve conflicts. However, later in life, the habit of running to one's parents to solve conflicts between siblings can become a problem known as "triangulation." Triangulation occurs when adults talk about feelings, opinions or personal issues regarding another person or a group with a third party instead of with the person or group actually involved. The only way to stop the triangulation is for each party to communicate their feelings, concerns and opinions directly to each other, adult to adult.

During communication triangulation in a family business or enterprise, people attempt to draw others into their own unresolved conflicts. Unless a person is asking another to help mediate a resolution, in which case the mediator hears both sides of the story, the person complaining is simply venting or gossiping. It's best to keep the focus on resolving the conflict by encouraging the two individuals to talk directly to one another. A three-way conversation can sometimes help, but only if the third party facilitates without taking sides, having a hidden agenda, speaking for one of the other parties or adding to the emotional drama in any way.

A great communication strategy is to avoid being recruited into a triangle in the first place. So often a well-intentioned third party realizes they have inadvertently let themselves be dragged into a disagreement, sometimes even into taking sides. Once you're caught in a triangle, escape is possible but may take some courage. A safer way of proceeding is to direct the person straight to the other individual involved. On the personal level, that's the only way for concerns to be addressed or a relationship to be mended.

Four important things happen once a venter learns that communication triangulation isn't allowed.

1) It signals to everyone that triangulation and side-taking are not acceptable behaviors.

2) By protecting the party not present, trust is built among the group, since others know that, if needed, the same thoughtfulness will be extended to them.

3) It demonstrates trust by the group that individuals embroiled in conflict will be able to resolve their own problems.

4) As family members accept that they are responsible for resolving their own problems, it allows family leaders and family business leaders to loosen their hold on the reins.

THE SCIENCE OF ANGER

In one of the families I work with, the family enterprise transition began with an explosive family meeting. I had been asked to join the meeting partway through so the family members could meet me and learn a little about my work as a family enterprise advisor. But when I entered the room, I felt as if all the air had been sucked out of it. I later learned that just before my entry a fourth-generation young adult family member had made an unexpected salary demand of the family-member-only business board. The discussion that ensued—heated, loud and angry—resulted in a request for a short recess so that some of the family members could calm their shaking nerves. A few days later, I learned from individual discussions with each family member that they were all troubled by what had happened, with those involved in the shouting match still feeling guilt, shame, embarrassment and frustration.

What could have helped them was some understanding of the science of anger. In a non-scientific nutshell, when anger is triggered, our brains produce chemicals that flood the brain's executive processes. Once those processes are flooded, our response becomes instinctual: fight or flight. In this family, it had been fight for some family members. Once an outburst has occurred, the chemicals recede in the brain, returning to normal levels, and the fighter—the yellers in this instance—often moves from anger to guilt, shame and/or embarrassment, in this case for having upset elderly family members so much that they needed to call for a recess.

There are bigger reasons why I share this science than to merely offer an understanding of what occurs chemically in our brains. One is to provide an opportunity for empathy and understanding for those who have heated emotional outbursts. The other is to allow people to understand that there is a way to prevent an emotional explosion and the guilt that follows. Since anger has a predictable path—trigger > explosion > guilt—the key to disrupting its path is not only to recognize our triggers but also to learn what it physically feels like to be triggered so we can choose a different path before the explosion.

When I met individually with the family members, I learned that each person was genuinely struggling with what had occurred. As they each recounted what had happened, I could see the physical reactions the retelling set off. One individual's eyes reddened, another's face flushed deep red. So, as each person exhibited a physiological reaction as they retold their version of events, I gently asked them to pause and tell me what they were feeling in that instant. This became a breakthrough moment for some of these individuals. As a result of what I was seeing—reddening watery eyes and a hot, flushed face—I drew their attention to what they could feel. They shared with me their discomfort of an increased heart rate before the chemicals completely took over, which resulted in uncontrolled outbursts in the past. In subsequent meetings, being aware of what they feel when they are triggered has allowed them to pause and change the course of their reaction. They are now working on avoiding defaulting into the anger cycle of trigger > explosion > guilt and instead practice a new pattern: trigger > deep breath > exercising curiosity by asking questions.

ROLE OF CULTURE

In my university days, I dated a fellow with a different cultural background from mine. At the first family dinner of his that I attended, I immediately noticed how family members communicated with great emotion and intensity, exploding and subsiding every few minutes. My own family's dinners were flat-line by comparison. While I was uncomfortable at first with the explosive dynamic at his family's dinner table, I soon realized it didn't reflect uncontrolled anger or destructive conflict. It was simply how this family communicated. The family's passionate way of communicating was neither better nor worse than my family's, just different. In fact, if my family had suddenly begun to communicate like his, or his like mine, it likely would have been evidence of a problem within their respective family systems.

WORDS DO MATTER

A generation of us grew up hearing the expression "Sticks and stones may break your bones, but words will never hurt you." All I can say is, that's just not true. Words can—and do—hurt. Freedom of speech is a right; it is also a responsibility. Yes, a responsibility! Be responsible with the words you use, because there are things that are almost impossible to take back. Some words, just like some actions, cannot be forgotten. Speaking honestly with kindness and empathy is different from speaking bluntly and unkindly. And when trust is low in a family, you need to be as conscientious and thoughtful about your choice of words with your family members as you would be on a first date.

FACE-SAVING

Face-saving can spare someone from embarrassment and protect their dignity. Allowing room for face-saving to happen in families is important in relation to trust. For instance, if a family member slips up in some way, publicly calling them out on the slip-up will deplete trust, while discreetly taking the person aside to explore what happened not only helps the individual but also builds up trust between the family members. Great leaders understand both the impact and the role of face-saving, and embrace this concept early in their leadership tenure.

ACTIVE LISTENING

Active listening is a profound act of respect and generosity. It is also a path to discovery that plays a vital role in building trust and strong communication within family enterprises. Active listening requires us to intentionally switch from the mode of being heard to that of listening: listening with all our senses to the words being spoken and also to the words not spoken, paying attention to the body language we see and the tones we hear (remember the work of Professor Mehrabian on page 49). It means pausing momentarily to let what we have heard settle in and then demonstrating curiosity through kindness, asking questions, choosing to be a seeker rather than a knower. It means listening without judgment, listening afresh, rather than hearing what we want to hear through the filter of what we believe to be true.

When we practice active listening, we discover there is seldom an absolutely right or wrong answer, and we are prepared to change our perspective. Listening like this allows for the birth of new ideas and builds and enhances harmony, knowledge and wisdom in the family enterprise. When we listen with open hearts and minds, we can hear the poetry, wisdom and grace in others. In a family enterprise, it lets each person know they are being listened to and have been heard, which in turn helps to build the bonds of trust and to strengthen relationships between family members.

MISSTEPS IN TRUST and communication are normal. Trust is strengthened when, as soon as we realize we've made a misstep, we own up to it and take corrective action. The best we can do is try, really paying attention to how and what others are communicating and then responding with clear intentions. That takes practice, practice and more practice, deliberate rather than autopilot communication, hanging in there when the going gets tough, remaining focused on kindness and empathy. When communication spins out of control, if you remember to pause, take a deep breath and consciously shift your reaction from judgment to curiosity, you and your family members will find yourselves deepening levels of trust and opening the door to possibility.

5

SHARED VALUES
AND VISION

THE SHARED values and vision your family members agree upon for your family enterprise are not mere words. They are a vital force in your multigenerational success. Representing who you are, what you stand for and what you collectively want to achieve, they are the rallying cry for current and future generations of the family. Most powerfully, they provide family members with a compelling reason to stick together and persevere as a united group through good times and bad. The task for every family enterprise is to unearth shared values and create a vision robust enough to energize your family to successfully pursue a seven-generation journey.

With families that grow in size through the generations, the increasing mobility of family members and the attendant likelihood of less direct family member involvement with the business, family enterprises need more than ever to have a clear understanding of their shared values and vision. Businesses may come and go in a family enterprise—and most certainly change—but the family's emotional connection to their shared values and vision lives on.

The articulation of shared values and a shared vision also has a harmonious effect on decision-making. When the decisions being made do not reflect a family's shared values and vision, trust is eroded and family harmony can be disrupted. When the decisions are anchored by the family's shared values and vision, however, there is a much greater likelihood of them being accepted by all family members. When family members agree with the decisions being made, family harmony is maintained, which helps to strengthen family unity. And as with trust, a family can never have too much harmony or unity!

The driving force in many successful multigenerational family enterprises isn't maximizing shareholder wealth or profits. Enterprises transitioning well into the second and third generations tend to have a core ideology that transcends purely economic considerations. Rather than simply pursuing profits, such enterprises are focused on pursuing the family enterprise's shared values and vision profitably. They recognize that profit is like oxygen: It is needed for the body to live, but it is not the point of life.

The money generated by a family business is like energy, a resource that flows in and out; it keeps the business going and the lights on. Your shared values and vision aren't affected by the amount of money your family enterprise earns. One family member earnestly said to me, "If we didn't have all this money, we wouldn't have these problems." But the truth is, money doesn't make things more difficult. In fact, to uncover a more deep-seated problem, consider this question instead: If there were no money involved, would you look forward to a dinner with your family members? What many families I've worked with discover is that money is the scapegoat they use to avoid difficult conversations.

The topic of values and vision seems to be a flavor of the month for consultants and the organizations they work for. Endless hours are spent, endless meetings are held—often with only management being consulted—to determine what a business stands for (its values) and what it wants to achieve (its vision). Often, though, these organizations don't quite get it right. That is especially evident when the actions of management don't align with the "shared values and vision" they announce to the rest of the organization. In the best-case scenario, when management's declared values and vision aren't evident in their decisions, their values and vision statements are ignored by the team they lead. In the worst-case scenario, the situation is demoralizing and destructive to team members. In both cases, an opportunity to lead a team to stand for something that inspires them to make a difference is lost.

As an example, at one time I worked in an organization that claimed its priority was to improve client service, something team members could get behind and passionately support. To achieve this, though, the organization developed questionnaires to send to randomly selected clients. After reading the questionnaire, it didn't take a rocket scientist to determine that the questionnaires were designed to extract more money from clients rather than improving client service. The natural result of management saying one thing and doing something different was for employees to distrust them and lose respect for their leadership.

In the family enterprises I deal with, it is common early in the process to find inconsistencies between the decisions being made and the family's articulated shared values and vision. These inconsistencies shouldn't be ignored. Trust and respect in the leadership of family enterprises are strengthened when the leadership actively listens to family members and addresses the disconnect between their actions and the family's shared values and vision.

I wish the same could have been said for the leadership of the organization I mention here. The disappointing result in that situation was not only the lack of active listening, despite the quantifiable surveys that had put this organization in last place in their industry for employee and client satisfaction, but also a leadership doubling down to defend their destructive decisions, seemingly disconnected from their stated values and vision and the people they led. Fortunately, the leadership in family enterprises can't hide inside the protective hierarchical cocoon of a large public company. Successful family enterprise leadership not only has to but also wants to be respectful of and curious about the concerns of the individuals they lead—that is, family members—at all times.

If the idea of a shared values and vision conversation is new to your family, then I suggest you have this discussion at your next family meeting. I recommend this for a number of reasons. One is that this is—or should be—a non-contentious topic because there are no wrong answers. Begin by giving family members two questions to think about before the meeting: "What do we stand for as a family?" And "What do we, as a family, want to achieve together?"

Asking these questions exposes many things to the light early on, letting you see what your next steps need to be. For instance, if family members can barely tolerate sitting at the same table, continuing to work through topics like the family's shared values and vision may not be possible. Getting a shared commitment to a long-term goal will not be easy in this kind of environment. And an upcoming ownership group who are unable to have conversations about their shared values and vision are not likely to have success with potentially more emotionally charged decisions like "the qualifications for earning a voice to become a decision maker or how to define family." Your options at this point, frankly, are limited to having family members consent to working with outside professionals like family enterprise advisors or conflict resolution coaches; letting disgruntled family members exit the family enterprise; or considering an all-out sale of the family business.

Shared Values

For the first meeting in which the topic of shared values is discussed, don't worry about the number of responses. Again, there are no wrong answers and the discussion will allow family members, sometimes for the first time in a family meeting setting, to practice their communication skills: speaking, sharing and listening as a team. Quite often the conversation prompts family members to see each other for the first time as the adults they have become, as opposed to the children they were. If at the end of the meeting your whiteboard has a hundred shared values on it, that's perfectly fine. It's a starting point.

At this stage, the process is as much about the ability to work together as it is about the output. However, the output itself might be interesting. Some of the families I've worked with struggle to distinguish between their core values, the ones they already have, and their aspirational values, the ones they aspire to. That's okay; it's great to have aspirations.

There is no need for perfection in this family conversation. Discrepancies between core and aspirational values will surface when the family starts making decisions. Sometimes something families thought they shared as a core value turns out to be a value they aspire to. This is quite common, and it's why the topic of shared values should be revisited at the start of each family meeting at the beginning of the process and later reaffirmed at least once a year.

As an example, I encountered a situation where the members of one family agreed that empathy was a core shared value. In this group, there were four siblings aged fifty-five to sixty-five who had worked for decades in four different branches of the family business. The parents unexpectedly decided to sell one of the businesses, which meant that the eldest sibling, who had a lifetime of service to that particular family business, was, through no fault of their own, going to be left unemployed, without a salary and without a pension. Although the entire family enterprise was exceptionally financially sound, some in the remaining sibling group believed that no ongoing compensation was necessary for this individual after that branch of the business was sold. Needless to say, the sixty-five-year-old sibling was concerned for their personal financial future.

Drawing attention to this family's shared values, I wondered aloud how eliminating the financial flow suddenly and unexpectedly to this family member was empathetic. The family discovered that empathy was actually an aspirational value, something they wanted to work toward, as opposed to a core value.

Fortunately, this situation was resolved and harmony was maintained as the family redefined the ways in which funds were distributed. In the past, funds had flowed only as salaries because all family members were employees. Going forward, the family established a compensation committee to consider other forms of family remuneration, including a dividend policy and a share buy-back program.

While each family will have its own specific shared values, here are a few values that are common to successful multigenerational families.

A COMMITMENT TO STEWARDSHIP

Stewards of the family enterprise, often members of a second-generation sibling group that has strong relationships with one another, are committed to exploring what it would take to extend the family enterprise across seven generations. A belief in stewardship comes from respect for the prior generations of family enterprise builders. Stewards see it as their duty to continue the family enterprise. They do not feel entitled to the family enterprise they inherit; they are instead humbled to be a part of a multigenerational journey. They believe strongly that their role is to handle with care the entire family enterprise for the benefit of family members they will never know. While determined and caring, stewards don't undertake this work for themselves; they do it for others.

Stewards know they are safeguarding not only the financial capital of the family business and the human and intellectual capital of the family but also the family's social capital: the trust built up through strong, bonded relationships within the family. Strong relationships between siblings make the family formidable; built up over generations, they can make the family enterprise invincible. It's common for long-united family members to feel a deeper commitment to the social capital they've earned through the generations than to the financial capital they've gained.

A GROWTH MINDSET

A growth mindset is a family's belief that their ability to do something isn't fixed, that they can change through learning. Successes and failures are a natural part of any multigenerational journey. When family members believe they can learn and change from their shared experiences, they increase their grittiness. And it's grittiness that will allow family members to pursue long-term goals like seven-generation family enterprise planning with passion and perseverance.

In today's rapidly changing world, a successful multigenerational family will not allow the family enterprise to be paralyzed by past processes. A growth mindset will set the entire family enterprise, including the family business, free. Like a puppy exploring every corner of a room, family members with this attitude stay open, abandoning judgment and pursuing curiosity. Families who commit to multigenerational planning constantly seek out information about ways to be successful and ways to bounce back from failures. Family members with a growth mindset believe they can do anything if they are willing to learn and remain committed to the task and the journey ahead of them.

RESPECT FOR THE LUCK FACTOR

There is typically a high degree of modesty and humility in successful multigenerational families. They quietly focus on their shared values and vision as opposed to tooting their own horns. Many appreciate that a degree of luck, or good timing, played a role in getting them to where they are. For instance, over my lifetime, I've witnessed a few core industries in my part of the world rise and fall. Sometimes a family business has the good fortune of being in a rising industry. In some cases, it can be said that the business builder in a specific industry was a visionary; in others, the domination of certain industries over the ages has often made no sense whatsoever.

And the same can be said for specific businesses making no sense and nevertheless being very successful. I remember a retail craze several decades ago that had people buying "pet rocks." Yes, pet rocks. A pet rock was literally a small rock sold in a small box. As long as the fad lasted, the owner of the business selling such items was, I believe, financially successful. On the other hand, many of us have known individuals who work diligently and effectively and yet their sound business ideas are not successful enough to survive.

I also believe there is a degree of luck associated with the capacity and willingness of upcoming generations to be part of a shared family journey. Family members are human, and humans sometimes defy our expectations. I've seen families bend over backward to encourage and inspire upcoming generations, only to find their efforts thwarted, and other cases where it hasn't made sense to me that family members would work unquestioningly together on a shared family journey, and yet they do. Parents can do all the "right" things or all the "wrong" things, yet the outcome is quite different from the one they expected. Such is the luck factor and the joy of parenting.

UNITY

Unified family members work together as a team, believing in the fingers-on-the-hand theory: Individually some may be smaller or bigger, stronger or weaker, but collectively they perform splendidly. United family members know they have to operate as a collaboration of skills, not a test of wills. They recognize that when they fight internally, their ability to compete externally is compromised.

Families like this understand, especially as the number of family members grows, that they will not always have unanimous agreement for the decisions made at meetings; instead, they work toward building consensus. Consensus means that no matter what, they are all 100% united behind any decisions made by the time they leave the decision-making table. This kind of support is essential to the stability of the whole family enterprise—the family and the family business.

Unified family members believe in kindness, but not in kindness without consequences. They know that unity depends on the actions of individuals. If intervention is needed with regard to the actions of a family member, they make a kind, constructive intervention as opposed to taking no corrective action, believing this to be the compassionate route for the family as a whole. Constructive, well-meaning feedback strengthens relationships, which fosters a united front all family members can support.

TRUST

Trust is a key ingredient in a successful multigenerational family enterprise. Without trust, everything else breaks down. And when there is no trust, the family enterprise, including the family business, is in trouble. This is a topic that comes up in all of the family meetings I attend. Family members will discover for themselves that trust is a family asset that can be built up or depleted. Families with high trust, I explain, work as hard at creating positive family relationships as they do at creating positive business relationships.

In building trust, family members should remain vigilant about role-modeling trusting behavior for upcoming generations. For instance, in one family I know, a family member who was preparing to be a future leader tried to grow the family business into new industries. Risks were taken, and the endeavors failed in a very public way, which made this upcoming generation member look foolish. However, while the media was ready and willing to disparage this upcoming family member, the senior family members who were sought out for public comment maintained their full support of this individual. They had this family member's back. Actions like that strengthen trust within a family.

Some family business leaders reject transparency and accountability because they do not want to share information. These leaders define loyalty as blind obedience. However, uncertainty and confusion can be reduced and trust strengthened when family members are communicated with regularly. Full transparent disclosure builds their understanding of the family business and family operations, making family members feel as if they are part of the family enterprise team. That builds confidence and trust between family members and better prepares upcoming generations and future owners.

Accountability is another necessary ingredient for building trust in multigenerational family businesses. Poor accountability for family commitments erodes trust within the family enterprise. But be careful when implementing accountability. Some families only use it in a potentially destructive way, calling out or punishing family members when they don't follow through on a commitment. Sadly, quite often these family members were doing their best and just had a slip-up. Remember, many entrepreneurs can reminisce about their slip-ups. Successful multigenerational family enterprises hold family members accountable in a proactive way, offering feedback and accountability checks for both good work and areas that need improving.

Shared Vision

Time and time again we hear that the family factor is the competitive advantage of a family business, but to say that is to fall short of the mark. It's not just family but the family's emotional commitment to their shared long-term journey that will drive the family's resourcefulness in reaching for its shared vision. In other words, what gets in the way of successful multigenerational family enterprises isn't a lack of resources but rather a lack of resourcefulness—the resourcefulness that family members tap into when they are passionately committed to their shared vision.

A family enterprise's shared vision starts with an interest in a shared journey and curiosity about what could be possible. Exploring the possibilities allows family members to figure out what they want to have happen and why. When they collectively address these questions, they discover that the best answer is the one that moves the family enterprise toward something inspirational and sustainable. When family members connect to the "why" behind their shared vision, the family as a unit is more likely to sustain the resourcefulness it needs to be successful over seven generations.

A shared vision will propel the family forward, allowing them to stumble while knowing they will keep moving forward. When families get their shared vision statement right, they are better able to handle both differences between family members and the uncertainty that is characteristic of today's rapidly changing world. Dealing with differences and uncertainties will require the passion and commitment that the family's shared vision inspires.

But I've not yet met a family who has landed on this kind of shared vision right from the start. Asking a family to articulate its shared vision is like asking a teenager what they are passionate about. Until teenagers know who they are and have had time to explore their interests, it's hard for most of them to clearly express their passions. In a family enterprise, it's difficult for family members to be 100% certain about what they collectively want to achieve until they've had time to explore what they stand for, their shared values and their interests as a group.

At the start, developing a shared vision is more about the process. The time family members spend having these conversations strengthens trust and communication. Some families start by reaching for some smaller shared goals, maybe in typically non-contentious areas like the family foundation or the family's community commitments. As family members continue to work together and revisit the topic, a compelling seven-generation shared vision can arise.

I WOULD BE DOING a disservice to successful multigenerational family enterprises if I didn't also mention the role of culture and traditions. The culture in a family is a reflection of the family's shared values and is typically proudly exemplified in the family business. Family traditions are evolutionary, stretching from the past through the present and into the future. Family traditions should be seen as guides, not leashes, bringing meaning and personality to the family enterprise that could otherwise easily be overlooked. So, keep this in mind and consider embracing family traditions. For instance, a group of second-generation siblings might grow up with the tradition of an annual family winter retreat to the tropics. As the family increases in number across generations, the location and the winter travel time may become impractical, but the intent of the tradition, strengthening family bonds and social capital, needn't be lost. Perhaps the gathering could be moved to a more accessible location and easier time of year for all family members, say the summer, and held every other year, reinforced with an annual family letter that updates everyone on everything.

Another aspect of family culture and traditions is the recording of the family history. By this I don't mean hiring a professional writer to capture Mom and Dad's stories, but having upcoming generations sit down with the older generations to ask the questions they are genuinely interested in hearing the answers to and discovering the older generations' stories. Recording your family history can be a very powerful tool by honoring the past, informing the present and reminding people about the future. Recording a family's successes and failures also gives the family a sense of identity, continuity and values.

ARTICULATING SHARED VALUES and a shared vision strengthens trust and communication among family members and provides the upcoming generation with clarity about what the family stands for and what it wants to achieve. You'll know you're on the right course when the conversation shifts from "I and me" to "we and us"; that's the start of changing the direction of the energy in the family enterprise. Once family members' perspectives evolve to embrace a multigenerational family enterprise, many families discover there isn't anything a group of dedicated family members can't achieve.

6

YOUR FAMILY ENTERPRISE:

Framework, Decision-Making and Policies

SOME FAMILY LEADERS cringe at the thought of creating a family enterprise framework, decision-making processes and policies, feeling they will strangle the entrepreneurial spirit that has been so instrumental in the success of their business. And yet, every family already has a way of organizing itself, making rules and setting boundaries. In the early days of building a business and the family's relationship with it, not much thought is given to this topic because the business and enterprise usually only has one owner, one controlling voice and one decision maker. However, in later generations there will be many owners, controlling voices and decision makers, and this means there's a strong potential for conflict and disharmony. By framing the way the business and family organize themselves, including decision-making processes and operating policies, multigenerational families are proactively managing the operations of the family enterprise in order for the family enterprise to succeed across seven generations.

In a typical family, the first-generation parents lead the family and establish rules and boundaries for the second-generation children to follow. This parent/child way of operating works well for a small number of closely related people, usually living under the same roof, with discussions and decisions being conducted via a family dinner table think tank. As the family expands in number and diversity to include spouses, third-generation cousins and generations beyond, trust, harmony and unity can be strengthened by creating a defined family enterprise framework, decision-making process and accompanying policies based on the family's shared values and vision. This approach increases the likelihood of a united, harmonious multigenerational family enterprise by:

· building trust and strengthening communication through the family working together,
· managing the expectations of upcoming generations by providing them with clarity about future potential roles and responsibilities, and
· solving some of tomorrow's predictable problems today—pay attention to this point.

Family meetings are the time and place to create your family enterprise framework and decision-making processes and policies. The time family members spend at these meetings articulating what they stand for and what they want to achieve together is valuable for several reasons. It gives family members the opportunity to practice their communication skills, especially if they are new to working together. It gives them a chance to build up some trust, which is reinforced when they recognize they all want the same thing. And it paves the way for harmony and unity in the family to be strengthened when the decisions made and the policies created align with the family's shared values and vision. In fact, families discover that the process of family members working together is as important as the actual family enterprise framework and decision-making processes and policies they create.

The more thought and care family members put into creating their family enterprise framework and decision-making processes and policies that work for them, the more successful the family will be in achieving its seven-generation planning goals. Family members are likely to abide by a framework, decision-making processes and policies they create themselves, rather than wasting time and resources fighting over a structure dictated by a family enterprise leader or an outside consultant. Additionally, by doing this work for themselves, they'll remain cautious about future changes to the processes and policies they developed, rather than changing them in response to a current whim.

As families enter this process for the first time, they discover a couple of things. The first is that the process is similar to building a business. Business builders seldom know exactly what steps they are going to take in building their business, but they do know what they want to achieve. Along the way they take some chances and make some risky decisions. When those risks prove successful, they press on; when they flop, the builders remain flexible and continue to adapt until success is achieved. They keep exploring and moving forward, iteratively building the business. They're gritty! The same goes for the activities family members enter into when creating their family enterprise framework, decision-making processes and policies.

Family Enterprise Framework

As the number of family member shareholders grows in size, maturity and diversity across the generations, a family enterprise framework is needed to ensure two things: that family members continue to make good decisions and that they know how they will organize themselves to get agreement on the decisions being made. A family enterprise framework, referred to by some as a governance structure, allows family members to make sound decisions while maintaining harmony and unity. (As I mentioned previously, I intentionally minimize the use of the word "governance.")

The process starts early with the business builders—the parents—having conversations with the upcoming generation—the siblings—about the family's shared values and vision and the purpose of the family business. As the upcoming generations mature, family members discover that while all businesses must be financially viable, businesses also exist for a variety of other purposes: providing work for business owners; meaning and purpose for their owners; connections to the community; livelihoods for stakeholders such as employees, suppliers and clients; pride and fun for the family, etc. When the upcoming generation understands early on the purposes of your family business beyond the financial returns, they will be more motivated to pick up the mantle of long-term planning.

As the sibling group reaches their late teens/early twenties, the first structure in your family enterprise framework will be your family meetings. The work at these meetings, as discussed, will include family members developing and practicing their skills in working together through conversations about the family's shared values and vision and about what will be required of family members if they want to earn a voice in future decisions made within the family enterprise.

During their mid- to late twenties, upcoming generation family members typically work on earning a qualified independent voice through continued education and/or jobs. They begin to learn and better understand why it's necessary to proactively manage the family's shared journey. This is also the time when the upcoming generation is learning about potential roles and responsibilities in the three different areas of the family enterprise: the family, family business ownership and family business management. When this work is being done in its early stages in a family that is composed of parents and siblings but whose future plans include all family members—that is, both the immediate and the extended family—having ownership interests in the business, it is common for family and family business ownership matters to overlap in these initial family meetings. However, to minimize the potential for disruption by family members not active in the family business, family business leaders are well advised to restrict discussions about family business management to those family and non-family members who actually work in the business.

Once the upcoming generation reaches their early thirties, the work at family meetings expands to include clarifying the group's shared values and vision, creating a family meeting code of conduct and then, in a progressive manner, working together to create an ownership pledge; a decision-making process; and policies concerning earning a voice, the definition of family, employment, compensation, conflict resolution, shareholder agreements, non-operating shareholders and pre-determination agreements, to name but a few things. If family members at the meeting table are reasonable, they discover these topics aren't necessarily complex. They also understand that creating policies today reduces the potential for emotionally based decisions in the future that could bring down the family enterprise, robbing future generations of a source of pride and connectivity.

By the time the upcoming generation are in their early to mid-thirties, and have been involved in creating some core policies for the family enterprise, they will be aware that specialized decisions need to be made regarding family matters, ownership of the family business and management of the family business.

However, the kind of family meetings in which family and family business ownership issues are intertwined, with a smaller group of closely related people—parents and children—working together, is seldom possible once the number of family members increases across generations and branches of the family. This is where the earned voice policy comes into play for each system, separating the decisions of the family and those of family business ownership that need to be made.

As a result, a family enterprise framework evolves to become a more formalized structure when the third and future generations begin to participate. Along with an increased number of family members will come an increased number of family members who meet the family's policy requirement to earn a voice. However, since too many voices can hinder rather than enhance decision-making, many families at this stage further separate family and family business ownership matters, perhaps calling the different groups something like the Family Council and the Ownership Board. They may put in place a policy that requires elections to be held among family members who have earned a qualified voice to fill the minimum and maximum number of seats on the Family Council and the Ownership Board.

By this multigenerational stage, the possibilities for different kinds of structures, or committees, within the family enterprise framework are endless, reflecting the unique shared values and vision of each family. For instance, a family that wants to encourage a strong entrepreneurial spirit in future generations might establish a Venture Capital Committee, in which members with an earned voice work together to allocate funds to family members pursuing entrepreneurial activities. Or perhaps the Family Council creates a Human Resource Committee that family members can approach for financial or emotional support to help them pursue independent purposeful lives, such as an education loan or a mentoring program.

Your family enterprise framework evolves in response to the changing needs of and growth in your family and your family business. Unique to each family, a family enterprise framework develops one meeting and one generation at a time.

Decision-Making

Family members who have earned a voice in decision-making often find there is no definitive right or wrong decision to be made. Many decisions often require having to choose between different options that have the potential to solve the same problem. These situations test the abilities of family members to work together. These decision makers must determine whether to be flexible or to stand strong, making certain they are not thinking only about themselves or the current generation but also about future family members.

Before I became deeply involved with family enterprises, I believed decision-making was a straightforward, democratic process in which reasonable people would gather, assess their options and then vote. The majority vote would win. I thought the only wrinkle was the need for a policy about a tie when an equal number of people were voting. So imagine my surprise when I kept coming across situations in which an odd number of reasonable, rational family member voters struggled to make reasonable, rational decisions.

For instance, take a family with three members in which two intelligent strong-willed individuals automatically pick opposite sides in any decision, leaving the third family member, let's call them the middleman, in the uncomfortable role of casting the tie-breaking vote. What if this middleman consistently casts their vote with the strongest-willed of these two individuals in order to avoid that person's wrath? For the larger family group, this is a disheartening, trust-depleting scenario in which the biggest bully at the table gets their way. Even worse, this can lead in general to decisions being made in an effort to tame the beast at the table as opposed to making the best decision possible for the long-term success of the family enterprise.

When the family factor is present, it can be very difficult to set emotions aside, even when approaching decisions with potentially far-reaching consequences for the wider group. Family decision makers may find themselves making an emotionally comfortable choice, like deciding to retain an underperforming family member as an employee even though this endangers the future of the family business and undermines the trust family members have in one another.

Another hurdle for sound decision-making in a family enterprise is fear of the unknown. In many cases, choices are hard not because family members lack insight, intelligence or information but because there is no clear right decision, only unknowns. The best thing in this circumstance is for family members to do their due diligence, document their process and then commit to a decision, while remaining flexible and adaptable if change is needed. The most important task for family members is to form a united front behind final decisions, all the while knowing they will make some mistakes over the course of the generations.

Successful multigenerational family enterprises who are proactive and commit to decisions get to be the authors of their future. Family members in decision-making positions do their homework, making certain they have the knowledge and insight needed to make the best decisions possible. They take their role seriously. As a result, they are in the driver's seat of their family enterprise's future rather than riding along passively and setting up the family enterprise for an unnecessarily bumpy ride.

A successful family enterprise needs a fair process for making decisions, especially when there is more than one decision maker. Fairness is defined both externally—by the processes and procedures a family enterprise establishes—and internally—by each family member's sense of being heard. If a decision isn't perceived as fair, it won't last. Family members who take the time to focus on how they're making decisions (that is, the process), rather than spending all their time on the decisions themselves, know this focus will make their family enterprise more efficient and improve the quality of the decisions being made. Family members gain confidence that things are fair and family unity is strengthened when they trust the systems and methods used to organize the decision-making process, even if they lose a vote from time to time.

There has been a lot of research in the area of decision-making, but here is the most successful, and perhaps the fairest, process I've seen work for family enterprises.

STEP 1: GET THE BEST VOICES AT THE TABLE

Determining who has a voice at the decision-making table might be one of the hardest decisions a family faces. Once made, however, it alleviates untold problems down the road. I'm always a little befuddled when a brilliant, visionary business builder allows all family members, or at least those past a certain age, to share their opinions on decisions under consideration when they have no qualifications except that of being blood relatives. Even worse, I see situations in which family members who have demonstrated over a lifetime that they are not even able to manage their own affairs still participating in a decision-making process that concerns the multigenerational aspirations of the family and the family enterprise. Since some of these individuals have not been offered even the most basic job in the family business, I'm left wondering why they are allowed a vote in the management or ownership of the family business. The hardest part is watching reasonable, qualified family members struggling to work with these individuals.

And disappointingly, I've witnessed these situations result in qualified family members who do have options exiting the family enterprise. That leaves the wanks, who not surprisingly don't have options in the outside world, in control.

For a group of family decision makers to work well together, they have to trust in one another's competency and abilities. They need to know all of the decision makers have earned a qualified voice, because qualified voices make quality decisions. To build trust, members of the group must spend time getting to know one another; they must respect one another's concerns and priorities before they can successfully make collective decisions. Good decision makers also get to know the other stakeholders in the family enterprise, respecting their concerns and priorities when making decisions that will have an impact on them.

STEP 2: SOLVE THE RIGHT PROBLEM

We are programmed to solve problems quickly. Too often, though, we go into our default mode, dealing with the presenting issue when a little digging would reveal that it wasn't the actual problem. As an example, two university students who share a dorm room are reaching the end of the semester and are low on funds. They go to their fridge, where they find one orange. They slice the orange in two, with each of them receiving half. Seems like a good decision, right?

Later, the peel from one half of the orange and the orange flesh from the other are tossed into the compost. You see, one person wanted the peel to make tea and the other wanted the flesh for eating. The students made a decision that solved the wrong problem. In family meetings, it's important to ensure you're solving the right problems, which often means beginning by checking in on your assumptions. For instance, do you consider that an orange is for tea making or for eating?

STEP 3: ASK BETTER QUESTIONS

Once you believe you're clear on the problem you're trying to solve, continue asking questions and exploring assumptions. Asking a better question can lead to a different answer, maybe even a better one. For instance, here's a common question asked in family enterprises: Should family members be required to work outside the family enterprise before working for the family business? Perhaps a better question is: What could be wrong with family members gaining outside work experience before joining the family business? These two questions are similar, but they take the information gathering in different directions.

If being in the role of asking questions, lots of questions, and exploring assumptions, yours and those of others, is uncomfortable for you, my advice is to take a break, give yourself time and space to think things through because stopping too early in the information-gathering and assumption-clarifying process can result in negative outcomes. For instance, years ago in my Conflict Resolution program I was asked to facilitate a practice dialogue between two family members who had to make a decision that they could both agree upon. During the facilitation, I found myself becoming very frustrated with one of the individuals because they had shut down, not speaking and not answering any of the, in my opinion, reasonable questions I was asking. In that moment, the non-speaking family member appeared unreasonable to me. Looking back, perhaps if I'd had my way in this training session, I would have walked away from that table having simply cast that individual into the role of "difficult" family member.

Even in the role of facilitator, I can still remember how overwhelmed and frustrated I'd become. As my level of frustration increased, my ability to ask a better question and explore assumptions being made decreased. The only solution I had was to ask for a break to clear my mind and think about what had happened in that conversation. When we reconvened,

I returned to the table with refreshed curiosity, prepared with better questions to ask and a focus on not labeling the "difficult" individual as such. In the end, I did discover why this role-playing family member had gone quiet, and was glad to have experienced this for the first time in a classroom rather than a real-life scenario.

If you're someone who has earned a voice in decision-making and you believe in any way there is more information to uncover and/or assumptions to clarify, do not give up. Sometimes all you need is to take a step away from the decision-making table in order to hit refresh and restart, which will help you create a new set of well-thought-out questions. You will then be in a position to gain the knowledge and insights you need to make an informed decision. And this is important, because making informed decisions will help you to avoid the three R's in decision-making: remorse, regret and resentment.

STEP 4: EXPLORE THE OPTIONS

It's important to recognize that there are no crazy ideas. All earned voices should be welcomed and encouraged. In order to open the minds of decision-making groups to alternative options, I recommend using something like a decision-making flywheel. This is where someone from the group stands at the front of the room and draws a large circle on a flip chart, drawing lines through it to divide it into eighths. As each option for a decision is suggested, the person at the flip chart enters it into one of the eighths, starting at the top and then progressing clockwise around the flywheel as options are offered. The option-generating exercise isn't complete until all the sections are filled, with the flywheel serving as a visual tracker.

In numerous meetings I've facilitated, some of the most powerful options have arisen when reaching the last one or two eighths of the flywheel. The first couple of solutions may spring forth easily, but the richness in exploring the family's options comes from continuing to add to perspectives and insights presented. When an idea is shared and recorded on the flywheel, try starting the follow-up response with "and" and not a "but." As noted earlier, "but's" kill ideas by shutting down curiosity. "And's" open the imagination to innovations or improvements. Bouncing around ideas has a way of becoming contagious, and as more of the group participates in such idea sharing, the possibilities expand exponentially. Strengthening your family's ability to explore all possible options is a valuable trait in any successful multigenerational family.

STEP 5: DECIDE ON A VOTING PROCESS

Every family will have a voting process that works for them. A simple majority vote when there is an unequal number of people works just fine. A majority vote can also work when there is an equal number of people, as long as you have an agreed-upon process to handle a tie.

For those exploring other voting models, here is a system that I've seen work well in multigenerational families. For our purposes, I'll call it the For/Against/Abstain/Object model.

A vote is taken. The number of fors and againsts is recorded in the minutes. The decision is made in accordance with the majority of the votes. Entering this process, each group leaves the table willing to accept the results of the majority. The abstain category is for individuals who have a conflict of interest or lack sufficient knowledge or information about the decision being made. By voting to abstain, they too agree to abide by the majority decision.

The objects are where it gets interesting. If even one person casts an object vote, the decision isn't passed. However, the individual who votes this way is then responsible for coming up with an acceptable alternative. The object vote should be used neither casually nor often, because family members are usually given plenty of notice to do their homework and work on their concerns prior to a decision being made. When it is, though, if an immediate alternative solution isn't provided by the objector, the objector is given a set amount of time to find an alternative solution—say thirty, sixty or ninety days—and a fresh vote. If there is still no resolution, one of two things happens. Either the objector takes the Quaker approach, letting go of their objection for the good of the whole, or a list of pros and cons regarding the subject under decision is prepared and delivered to a pre-determined trusted body for arbitration, perhaps the family business advisory board or a council of respected elders.

One last note on the decision-making process. Many families also include guidelines as to what kind of decision-making process and what level of support are required for different kinds of decisions. For instance, decisions that could result in changing a previously agreed-to policy, approving capital expenditures greater than a certain amount or agreeing on a merger, acquisition or disposition might require a decision-making process like the one described above but with more than a simple majority support—say, greater than 90% support. And other decisions, such as voting on where the family's annual meeting will be held, may only require simple majority support.

STEP 6: PRESERVE UNITY

What goes on in the boardroom stays in the boardroom. When the final decision has been reached and the decision makers leave the room, the vote may not have been unanimous but there is 100% consensus reached via a robust and agreed-upon decision-making process. Maintaining family unity is a key value of successful multigenerational families, and part of that is presenting a united front. This offers stability not only to the family members, thereby strengthening trust and belief in the decision makers, but also to the employees of the family business. It is remarkably damaging to the stakeholders in a family enterprise when the decision makers are warring publicly with one another.

Policies

The most successful policies of a family enterprise are the ones members create for themselves. Trust and unity are strengthened when policies are something family members have a say in and agree to abide by. Policies also stand the greatest chance of being seen as fair when they reflect the family's shared values and vision, including having earned, qualified voices at the table where the policies are being created.

In a multigenerational family enterprise, the goal is to create big-picture policies that are both current and forward-looking in an attempt to address both immediate challenges and the predictable problems of tomorrow. The minutes from the meetings in which these policies are created should document the thought process and reasoning that went into the creation of each policy, as well as recording the final decision. This will allow future generations to be well informed if, years down the road, consideration is given to changing the policy. For instance, first-generation business builders and owners may have had a policy that prohibited the family from taking funds out of the family business for any purpose other than financing the operating costs of the business. However, later generations may believe there is a need to set aside funds from the business to create, when financially feasible, a separate pool of capital for potential share redemptions by family members who choose to no longer be owners of the family business.

Additionally, by creating policies to address predictable issues in a family enterprise before they are needed, as opposed to after the fact, you can avoid the potential for emotionally driven decisions that other family members can sometimes experience as personal attacks. Even if these issues never arise, going ahead and creating policies will have given family members a chance to practice making decisions as a group. That will make them better prepared to deal with unexpected decisions in the future.

As a starting point, here is a list of some predictable issues that are worth considering creating policies for today.

EARNING A VOICE

With an earning-a-voice policy, based on the knowledge that qualified voices make quality decisions, the decision-making process can be remarkably seamless.

As noted in previous chapters, the earlier you create an earning-a-voice policy the better, because such a policy is effective in managing the expectations of upcoming generations. It removes the belief that all family members have a "right to" or are "entitled to" a voice in family enterprise decisions. Otherwise, family members who see their names on a corporate organization chart as shareholders, an ownership interest most often created as a result of tax planning, may suddenly have an opinion they feel should be heard and acted on by the family enterprise. The fallout can be disastrous when these individuals have no expertise or ability to play nicely with other family members and are focused solely on their own needs.

If the first generation doesn't establish an earning-a-voice policy, I strongly recommend this in the second generation, preferably before the third generation exists, or at least while they are still toddlers. This allows the second generation to create a policy that can't be interpreted as being directed at specific family members.

Deciding which qualities are required for earning a voice, and then applying these parameters to family members, might be one of the toughest moves for any generation. The list of required traits may seem more qualitative than substantive, and that means that applying the policy will require a sensitive and nuanced approach.

For decisions that involve the multigenerational success of the family enterprise, the required qualities for decision makers might be something like the following:

· Is able to work harmoniously with other family members.
· Is able to put the needs of the whole family ahead of their personal needs or those of their own branch of the family.
· Is financially independent from the family, or has the ability to be.
· Has earned the respect of family members through their accomplishments outside of the family.
· Shows respect to family members, especially the older generations.
· Is able to work consistently and kindly toward the resolution of differences of opinion.
· Is open-minded and willing to admit when they are wrong.

Your own list of qualities will reflect your individual family enterprise and the needs of its three systems: the family, family business ownership and family business management. Be clear about your intentions and explain why you believe certain qualities are necessary. Remain flexible in applying the policy, especially with regard to younger family members; they may look as if they'll never be candidates for earning a voice, but people mature, and the same person might be quite different at thirty-one than they were at twenty-one. Whatever you decide is needed in your earning-a-voice policy, be compassionate and resolute in its application.

DEFINING FAMILY

This is a topic that needs serious consideration—and again, the earlier the better. We're long past the days where family can be defined simply as blood relatives through a single marriage.

Some families still choose this definition, but today, in the twenty-first century, in other families the definition is often expanded to include adopted children, stepchildren and family members in long-term non-marital relationships. Some families may question whether children are still family members if their parents divorce.

One family I worked with decided to explore the meaning of family by having everyone write down their definition of family, then shuffling those definitions and handing them to me. I read each one aloud, and a group discussion followed. Once everyone had their thoughts, concerns and ideas listened to, a consensus was reached. That group, in alignment with the family's shared values and vision, believed a more expansive definition of family was the route to go. They felt that a larger pool of candidates to draw upon for earning a voice would help them find more creative solutions to problems in the future and, therefore, to make even better decisions—elements that would further strengthen their chances of creating a successful multi-generational family enterprise.

EMPLOYMENT OF FAMILY MEMBERS

The odds are high that you'll eventually have a family member wanting employment in the family business. In the normal course of things, businesses are accustomed to employees stepping up and succeeding in their jobs; if not, they fire them. This can cause problems for families who haven't thought in advance about what to do if a family member doesn't measure up to the job requirements. Creating a policy for this well in advance will give the group a chance to practice their decision-making skills, even if the policy is never needed. And such a policy can help you avoid headaches in the future, when heat-of-the-moment responses could result in an underperforming family member seeing a decision as a personal attack of some kind.

A good employment policy is thoughtfully planned out, carefully monitored and objectively implemented. As a general proposition, it will enable the family business to hire the most talented individuals, which will increase the effectiveness of the entire family enterprise. However, employment policies are as unique as the families who create them. One family may have hard-and-fast rules against family employment, allowing no family members to work in the family business. Another may draft a policy based on meritocracy, whereby family members are treated in the same way as outside candidates when they apply for jobs. Some families believe in nepotism, with the family always coming first; they believe in the saying "Success is relative, and the closer the relative, the greater the success."

When creating an employment policy, start with your family's shared values and vision, and then make a pros and cons list regarding your employment policy guidelines to address areas of risk. For instance, consider the potential impact on the family enterprise of a family member being handed a role rather than first working outside the business in order to earn that role. Competence isn't inherited, it's learned.

On the pro side, many positives will come to light. A family member with experience independent of the family business, especially if they've had a couple of promotions, has demonstrated to themselves and others that they have the grittiness to get the job done. If they join the family business and for whatever reason can't continue, they'll have something to fall back on. And when family members work independently, it means they aren't looking at the family business as the only way to meet their personal financial needs. Family members who are capable of standing on their own two feet, emotionally and financially, often add the greatest value to the family business and gain a respected voice in the family and/or family business ownership.

The only significant con I've come across in terms of this question is the concern that a family member may choose not to join the family business because they are enjoying working outside the family business. To this I would say, if a family member finds somewhere else to work that fills them with joy and purpose, then well done in setting these family members free. Remember, even if they aren't working in the family business, if they've earned a voice, that voice will be invaluable at the family and family business ownership tables.

If you are a family member who earns the opportunity to work in the family business, be aware that in most instances extra will be required of you. Non-family members will be watching, so act with integrity and remain loyal and respectful to your family and supportive of the family business and all the stakeholders. Keep in mind that all rules and boundaries that apply to non-family members also apply to you. For instance, a non-family member is not allowed to tamper with their time records—and neither are you! If special opportunities come your way simply because you're a family member, be certain to handle them (if you can't get out of them) with humility and gratitude. Just as elsewhere in life, not all employees will like you, but you can earn respect by monitoring and managing your own behavior.

Employing a spouse in the family business is another topic that needs to be considered. If the marriage breaks down, would that be awkward? If the spouse is a key, trusted employee in this scenario, does that make a difference? If the spouse worked at the family business before meeting and marrying one of the family members, does this affect the decision if something goes wrong? A family member dating an employee of the family business may allow the employee access to confidential information. What would be the policy for such a case? There are no right or wrong answers to any of these questions;

there are simply things to consider, different options and many more questions. Creating an employment policy is about exploring ideas, discovering common ground and making decisions that best reflect your family's shared values and vision.

COMPENSATION POLICY

You might be surprised to see this topic included since, like so many experts in the field, you can't imagine why it would be contentious. Surely most families and family businesses strive to offer a fair wage for the job done? However, my observations have shown me something quite different. In one instance, a family member working in the family's privately controlled and publicly traded company requested higher pay. The compensation committee of the board of directors decided that the family member did not deserve a raise, but felt that the first-generation family leader, the chair of the board, was grossly underpaid. A decision was made to give the chair a pay raise—which he promptly passed on to the family member whose request had been declined. It was an interesting solution on the family leader's part. However, it was also one that undermined the trust of other family members in the family enterprise's compensation policies.

In another situation, once family members started discussing openly how the family leadership allocated money to adult family members, major unresolved issues were unearthed and questions around fairness and equality were raised. In this instance, where trust was high and communication strong, family members were able to overcome the differences in financial distributions to family members. They understood that family leaders—in this case, the parents—aren't perfect but make the best decisions possible with the information they have. In this situation, the parents had not intended to be unkind or to show preferential treatment; they were trying to be helpful by responding to family members in financial need.

Family members who have earned a job in the family business should be compensated fairly and appropriately, just as non-family employees are. Most sustainable family businesses have comprehensive compensation policies that disallow special exemptions, either higher or lower, for family members. And it's important to remember that *fair* and *equal* are not the same thing. In one family, in order to maintain equality, all family members working in the family business were paid the same amount. The problem was that one family member worked only six weeks a year while the others worked fifty-two weeks a year. Over decades, this unfair policy had a number of unintended consequences, including the buildup of deepseated resentments and a false sense of worth and security developing in the individual who was being vastly overpaid.

An often-overlooked compensation policy addresses qualified family members who are not employees of the family business but provide time and expertise to the family enterprise by serving on or being elected to roles with responsibilities: Family Council, Owners' Council, Human Resource Committee, Venture Capital Committee, Investment Committee, etc. A fair compensation policy should reflect the importance of these roles in the future success of the family enterprise. Resist the urge to underpay people because "it's family." That can lead to a policy that encourages weak family members to be involved and discourages the best and brightest.

In addition, be cognizant of members in multigenerational families who are doing work that often goes unrecognized. The family business leader receives compensation and recognition, but the people working tirelessly at cooking, cleaning and organizing annual family retreats are doing the heavy lifting of holding the family together. Because their role of holding the family together is as important as that of the CEO holding the business together, their work should also be appreciated and, if possible, compensated.

CONFLICT RESOLUTION

Differences of opinion are normal, and they are to be expected when there is more than one decision maker in the family. Families who agree on a process for resolving conflict long before it's needed will have the greatest success in maintaining unity in the family. The intent of a policy like this is to capture how the family enterprise will deal with a difference of opinion. In terms of a specific process, families may turn the issue that's causing conflict over to a trusted family business advisory board or a group of respected family elders or hire outside professionals to arbitrate instead. If the policy names specific trusted individuals, then a process should also be established for updating the list as people retire or age out. With today's much longer life expectancies, some families have discovered when they've gone to apply the policy that a trusted individual named in it no longer has the mental capacity they did when the policy was created. Remember, the best meals lawyers have are on the backs of someone else's conflict. Get a policy in place.

ACTIVE/NON-ACTIVE FAMILY MEMBER SHAREHOLDERS

It is reasonable to assume that as your family grows, there will be family member shareholders who are not active in the family business. It's to the advantage of the active family members to work with these non-active members, because when the two groups are united, the likelihood of success for your family enterprise is far greater.

When dealing with issues regarding non-active family shareholders, it is important to make clear distinctions between family business ownership and family business management. It can be troublesome when family shareholders interfere with the management of the family business. However, non-active family shareholders who have earned a voice can be valuable allies for the family business, especially in areas where they have independent expertise.

Active family business shareholders will strengthen trust and unity with the non-active family shareholders when they treat them as valued partners. Trust and unity continue to be strengthened through strong communication in all matters concerning the family business, including financial results and financial distributions. In addition, it is useful for everyone to be clear on what the potential levels of involvement for all shareholders might be. Like active family members, non-active family shareholders must earn a voice. Once they have, however, they should not be excluded from meaningful participation.

The potential for problems exists if a tiny minority of non-active family members slips into the role of being vocal complainers. This can be avoided if active family member shareholders find ways to involve non-active family members in the family enterprise—for instance, by holding a family meeting at least annually to reaffirm the family's shared values and vision; by welcoming non-active shareholders to participate in conversations at the family table; by being open and transparent about the family business; by being clear about your family enterprise framework, decision-making processes and policies; by being accountable for and cognizant of issues related to power and status; and by allowing non-active family members to strive for defined roles in the family enterprise, such as members of the Family Council, the Ownership Board or special task forces like the Venture Capital or Human Resource Committees.

In the end, a policy that clearly lays out the relationship of non-active shareholders—shareholders who are not working in the business—to the family business is advisable. That might sound like overkill, but I witnessed a situation where a family shareholder who didn't work in the family business, had not earned a voice and was entirely financially dependent on the family called the non-family business management with a personal request and said, "Don't you know who my daddy is? He owns the business!" This kind of behavior is more common than you might think and it puts those on the receiving end of this kind of behavior—non-family management in this example—in an awkward position and embarrasses the rest of the family. Many people, of course, think that such a thing would never happen in their family—but it does; maybe not in the current generation, but as the number of family members grows across the generations, the likelihood of such an event increases. Therefore, please consider a policy that governs the behavior of non-active shareholders in relation to the family business, including consequences if the policy isn't followed.

SHAREHOLDER AGREEMENTS

The first thing to consider when creating shareholder agreements is whether you are willing to allow family shareholders who no longer wish to be owners in the family business to sell their shares. This is entirely your decision, but having been through it myself and with other family enterprises, I believe it is a waste of the family's valuable time and energy to battle internally with an unhappy family member shareholder rather than focusing on the external headwinds challenging the family business. When the family enterprise has the opportunity to set loose its angry, trapped critics, it can strengthen the remaining family member shareholder group. Families whose policies provide an exit clause actually have a greater retention rate of family members choosing to stay connected with the family enterprise. Another way to look at it is this: Without the choice of ownership, there can be no real commitment.

In most cases, family members become family business shareholders in the second generation, as a result of tax and estate planning. My best advice is to create shareholder agreements that manage the ability to buy or sell shares at that time. In cases where shareholder agreements are not executed at the time the shares are created, consider creating a shareholder agreement while family members still view their share ownership as a gift. It is easier to create a policy that allows family members to leave with dignity and a sense of fairness at that point rather than waiting until they view their shareholdings as a right or entitlement and you find yourself in a hostage situation. A fair exit agreement can help to ensure continued healthy family relationships.

This may go without saying, but creating this policy well in advance also allows the family to proactively consider their shareholder liquidity and redemption program, and the valuing and funding of it. This means that if a family member requests that the family business buy back their ownership shares, the business has a way of determining value and the request will not bankrupt the family business or leave it in financial harm's way.

A final note to family members considering selling their shares in the family business: Think twice about your decision. If it's being done to finance your short-term lifestyle benefits, selling your heritage may not be the right move. Your decision affects not only you but also your descendants and their future rights and involvement. Once your shares are sold, it's very unlikely you and/or your descendants will be able to get back in as shareholders.

PRE-DETERMINATION AGREEMENTS

Every marriage comes to an end, by either divorce or death. You, not your family, chose your spouse. Therefore, when your marriage comes to an end, a pre-determination agreement deals with your shares in the family business. While families may support a family member's freedom to choose their spouse, they don't necessarily choose these spouses to be a shareholder in the family business. A pre-determination agreement specifies what happens to your shares in the family business if you should predecease your spouse or if you and your spouse divorce.

NO ONE SIZE fits all family enterprise frameworks. In fact, as your family members and your business grow and mature, your family enterprise framework will change, along with the decision-making process and policies you have created. Some families ask when the best time is to start this work to increase the odds of success. My answer is that any time is a good time to start, maybe tonight at the family dinner table think tank, especially if the focus is on strengthened communication and trust in the family and on family conversations regarding the family's shared values and vision. Conversations about the specific needs of individual family members and the business will evolve over time.

In a family business transition plan, it is advisable for the first generation to encourage the upcoming generation, the sibling group, to create decision-making processes and policies largely on their own, perhaps with the assistance of a family enterprise facilitator. This is because the upcoming generation will have to live with the results. Additionally, each time they gather to work through issues and make decisions that create policies, they will be strengthening communication and trust. Since some of their decisions will be successful and others not, they will also learn that together they can survive setbacks, hit the restart button and begin again. Each challenge they face together and work through together will make them better prepared to successfully handle the next challenge. The result will be that they will grow confident they can solve problems rather than letting problems pull them apart.

Once the second generation is up and running, much of the work for the third and future generations will be in place, with an accepted family enterprise framework, decision-making processes and agreed-upon policies. The role of the third and following generations is to continue to nurture the family as a source of stewardship, responsibility and commitment for the three key groups in a family enterprise—the family, family business ownership and family business management—with the goal of transitioning the family enterprise from one generation to the next.

AS KYLE (Mackenzie Kyle) indicates in his book *The Performance Principle: A Proactive Guide to Understanding Motivation in the Modern Workplace*, be aware of the "scorpion effect." In other words, the intent of the work I describe here is to get an effective family enterprise framework and policies in place so that no matter how careless family members are, they can't sting themselves. The journey toward creating your family enterprise framework and policies is not about perfection; it's as much about the practice experienced by family members as they work through these processes as anything else. Trust, harmony and unity will be strengthened as your family learns to work together to create the strongest family enterprise possible. As my husband, Paul Hamilton, says, being successful at this work is similar to being successful at hockey: it takes preparation and practice. After all, you don't want to show up to the game with unsharpened skates, unable and unprepared to play with your teammates.

7

THE ELEPHANT
IN THE ROOM

T HE PHRASE "the elephant in the room" refers to an unresolved matter or taboo topic that is obvious to everyone
in an assembled group but is being deliberately avoided. You
all know there is an elephant and it is in the room, and it isn't
one of those cute cartoon elephants. Many family leaders find
dealing with such elephants one of their greatest challenges.
Even leaders who can do what needs to be done to build a glob-
ally successful business may still struggle to do what needs to
be done when it comes to the elephants in the room. But these
elephants must be confronted, because they can sabotage the
future success of a multigenerational family enterprise, even
if a family has developed a strong family enterprise framework,
sound decision-making processes and solid, family-agreed-
upon polices. This chapter offers some ideas about how to manage elephants in the room. Exciting!

In families where there is no family business, exhausted or
overwhelmed parents may avoid contentious family matters to
stave off an embarrassing or awkward conversation or an argu-
ment. If the elephant in the room involves a difficult younger
family member, parents may choose to "keep the peace." This

approach is understandable, since families have to survive their state of togetherness only until the children reach early adulthood, and then family members are theoretically free to pursue their independent lives. But in families whose members will one day collectively steward a multigenerational family enterprise, parental actions taken today to "keep the peace" may undermine long-term unity and trust.

While it may be more convenient to do the easy thing in the moment, for the success and well-being of a multigenerational family, it's best to do the right thing in the first place. "Keeping the peace" actions often involve parents giving in to the demands of the loudest, angriest bully at the dinner table. However, this kind of acquiescence can allow early problems in a family system to set in. Once a pattern is established, it is harder to undo, and siblings can learn at an early age how to work the family system to their individual benefit. Peace-keeping actions can have a negative impact on other family members too, as they may cause them to believe that the rules created by the family only apply to certain family members or that those rules can be broken. This breaks their trust in the family system. And the unfairness inherent in individual "keeping the peace" actions can lead to long-term resentments among family members, also depleting trust.

Your family enterprise will be successful over the long term when you remain flexible and adaptable in the decisions you make. Whether you are dealing with unresolved matters, taboo topics or difficult family members, you will make some good decisions and some not-so-good decisions. However, as a family enterprise leader, you are always allowed to change your decisions, including when they aren't working with regard to the elephant in the room. In fact, you *must* change them for your family enterprise to remain successful and relevant over multiple generations. When taking what feel like bold steps regarding the elephants in the room, be kind to yourself and to others, keeping in mind two very important things: You are doing the best you can with the knowledge you have, and you're not responsible for the choices or personal decisions made by others.

Role of the Elephant Herder

There's a reason the common expression refers to the *elephant* in the room, not the *mouse* in the room. While everyone notices an elephant in the room, they may not notice a mouse. Often, what starts as a small issue gets bigger and scarier as time passes, moving from inconsequential or mildly irritating to annoying, frustrating and ultimately intolerable. In other words, ignoring an issue doesn't make it go away. It's up to the family enterprise leader to demonstrate leadership by identifying and addressing the elephant in the room. Failing to do so can injure not just the family business and all its stakeholders but also current family members and future generations.

In a business that is not family-controlled, successful leaders deal with elephants either themselves or through the organizational systems in place. If the elephant is an employee, that person is held accountable for their actions. The same cannot always be said of leaders in a family-owned business, or of the systems in a family enterprise. Family members may not be held accountable for their actions, and uncomfortable conversations within the family may be avoided. Over time, however, as noted, inaction can lead to resentments and a depletion of trust in the family enterprise, threatening family unity.

Undiscussables

Undiscussables are taboo topics within a family or issues that start as a problem between two family members, then spread through the group, causing side-taking in the rest of the family and even in the family business. The result can be family members who are unable to work together to make reasonable decisions. I appreciate that undiscussables exist for powerful reasons. They are prickly on the outside, a bit like a porcupine, which makes them difficult to approach. But by leaving them unaddressed, you risk continuous intense conflict between family members that can crush the productive energy of your family enterprise.

Undiscussables are unique to each family enterprise in their content, but they tend to have a predictable trajectory over time. Deb Houden, PhD, and Wendy Sage-Hayward captured this brilliantly in their article "Undiscussables: Dealing with the Elephants in the Family Business" as:

· SILENCE: The irritated person fails to speak up about an issue or irritant. Since the irritator is often unaware that anything has happened, there's a missed opportunity to work through the issue.

· FRUSTRATION: The irritated person becomes increasingly upset if the irritant is ongoing and there is still neither recognition nor resolution of it.

· RESENTMENT: By now, the story behind the initial irritant is embedded and a resolution of the issue seems unattainable. Trust starts to be depleted as resentment builds and relationships weaken.

· CONFLICT: With no solution or resolution in sight, the situation escalates to conflict, either open or behind the irritator's back. One outcome is a weakened decision-making process, because family members don't trust each other enough to effectively work together.

· UNRESOLVED LONG-TERM CONFLICT: What began as one unresolved issue boils over into other areas of the family. By now, the entire family has often been drawn into the conflict. The resulting tension threatens family unity and the ability of the family to enjoy one another's company.

· LAWSUITS AND THE POTENTIAL LOSS OF THE FAMILY BUSI-NESS: Because of poor leadership, warring factions within the family eventually turn to lawyers to solve their issues.

I've watched all six of these steps play out on more than one occasion. In one situation involving four siblings aged between sixty-five and seventy-five the initial issue had occurred between two of them when they were teenagers. (I mention it earlier in the book—the issue was "You stole my boyfriend.") When I heard the story, various thoughts passed through my mind, including, "Wow, what an issue to choose to hang onto for almost six decades" and then "Imagine if the person with the capacity for that kind of intense commitment to an issue had chosen to focus this commitment on working with, rather than against, their fellow family members." (My third thought was that this teenage boy must have been pretty darn special!) Sadly, the trajectory from silence through resentment to lawsuits wasted energy and opportunities for this family enterprise.

Conflict

Fear of conflict is one of the big reasons family members avoid the elephant in the room. I can fully empathize with this, as for most of my life I believed conflict had to be loud, angry and a little terrifying. However, I've come to understand that it is nothing more than a difference of opinion. In fact, a good example of the power of words in strengthening communication comes when we replace the word "conflict" with the phrase "difference of opinion"—one sounds like arming up for battle, and the other sounds like a necessary part of the process in making good decisions. A family enterprise that wants to remain vigorous over multiple generations won't settle for the status quo in today's rapidly changing world. Encouraging family members with earned voices to offer different opinions, ideas and perspectives will enhance the long-term prospects of the family enterprise. The elephant already looks friendlier.

So, the first thing to recognize is that there *will* be conflicts, or differences of opinion. Some of them will have to do with the family and others with the family business. One difficulty to watch for is conflict being acted out in the wrong arena. Most families have issues to work through, and the family business can become an inviting, yet inappropriate, forum for their perpetual reenactment. For instance, the sibling who was aggrieved over the stolen boyfriend from decades prior carried her anger and distrust into the family business. During a discussion at the decision-making table regarding the salary being paid to her son, she injected statements like "You messed with my boyfriend, now you're messing with my grown son. You never liked me or my family!"

Communication experts have identified five differing conflict styles:

· Directing
· Avoiding
· Accommodating/harmonizing
· Compromising
· Collaborating/cooperating

Research indicates that each of us leans predominantly toward one or two of these styles, though we may all exhibit a little of each. None of these styles is better or worse than the others, and each has its pros and cons. For instance, in a time-sensitive situation such as a battlefield, a Director—as in "Move now or die!"—is preferred over an Accommodator—as in "No, no, you first."

Just knowing about these styles might give you some insight into why some elephants act the way they do—which can help you, the elephant herder, move from frustration at and judgment of the individual in question to understanding and appreciation. For instance, in one family I work with there are five children. The oldest sibling has a high-powered job independent of the family business. I have noticed that on occasion at family meetings this sibling exhibits a Director style. I've also noticed that their directness sometimes annoys other family members or makes them uncomfortable, but they serve a valuable role by voicing what needs to be said. Upon reflection, this family has learned to be grateful that this member is willing to take the heat by initiating tough conversations and asking the hard questions.

A Director, however, should not be confused with a bully at the table. A bully at the table is someone who has honed, over their lifetime, the ability to turn the family enterprise system upside down. While working with one family, who didn't have a policy for earning a voice, I noticed a pattern emerging. When a certain adult family member didn't get their way, they manipulated the process in a manner similar to a two-year-old kicking and screaming in the middle of a supermarket until they get the cookies they want.

In this situation, the person would first make an unreasonable request. When no acceptance followed, their voice would rise as they made their request more loudly. If there was still no acceptance, anger and threats would follow, and the next phase would be tears, accompanied by comments like "You don't understand me; you've never understood me! You don't love me." At this point, when the exceptionally kind and empathetic family members were occasionally able to remain resolute, the bully at the table would bring out the big gun, launching an attack on their fragile elderly parents, who were also seated at the table. At this stage, the other family members would reluctantly give in to protect the parents. Needless to say, as long as this family gives in to the bully's tantrums, poor decisions will continue to be made.

Because differences of opinion are predictable, and trust, unity and harmony are critical to the success of a multigenerational family enterprise, the strongest advice I can offer here is that you must expect conflict and, when it arises, do not avoid it. Differences of opinion in a family enterprise can be largely managed with a solid earned voice policy. There is a big difference between the bully at the table and a family member who has earned a voice and has a different communication style from your own and/or the rest of the family's.

Family Members as Elephants

As noted, for family leaders, it can help to understand what might be going on for family members who are elephants in the room. For instance, sometimes the loudest, angriest elephants at the table are family members with low self-worth. Self-worth is further diminished, however, when families jump in and save these family members, except in life-threatening situations. Doing so robs these individuals of the opportunity to build self-esteem and learn what they are capable of. Further, family members with low self-esteem who haven't earned their voice at the table through their own hard work, intelligence and perseverance sometimes end up being the elephants who don't respect and can be resentful of those who have.

Another elephant in the room can be the entitled family member. This is the person who demands benefits they haven't earned. Entitlement too often grows out of insecurity and low self-worth, and parents can unintentionally create entitlement issues if they teach their children they automatically deserve what their parents have earned. This egalitarian approach can backfire, because when children haven't earned those things, they make no connection between effort and reward.

An elephant can also arise when parents and children believe that fair must mean equal. If there are six siblings in the second generation, it's highly unlikely that they can all be CEO of the family business. It will also be detrimental to the business if all six siblings are allowed a voice in decision-making even though one of them, for instance, has demonstrated a lifetime of poor decisions, troubled family and personal relationships, ongoing business failures and difficulty with police and tax authorities. Equality might look like this individual having a one-sixth voice at the family enterprise table, but in no way is that fair to the other family members, the family business or the entire family enterprise. A strong earned voice policy will prevent this from arising too.

Elephants versus Problems

When approaching the elephant in the room, the goal is to separate the person from the problem. If you launch an attack on the elephant, they are likely to get defensive and charge. If you don't want the elephant to trample your family enterprise or other family members, or potentially get in their own way, I recommend approaching with genuine compassion and curiosity. This will require active listening and the asking of respectful questions grounded in a desire to figure out what is happening.

As you, the elephant herder, explore what's going on for the elephant, stay focused on fixing the problem, not the person. It's not a family leader's job to fix people. A family leader is most successful when they approach the elephant in the belief that the elephant isn't broken but rather there is a pattern that isn't working for them. As you start asking questions and really listening to the answers, including those that shed light on assumptions that are being made, you will likely get a different reaction from the elephant, moving in their mind from adversary to ally. What I find interesting is that, when you switch to this approach, you may well discover that the person who has been labeled the elephant, or the troublemaker, is actually the truth teller, perhaps the only person direct and brave enough to bring up the family's undiscussables.

You can't work with someone to resolve a problem if you don't know what the problem is. In some cases, you may find that you can't get an answer even to your most caring and empathetic questions. When this happens—and it is not uncommon—please remain patient. Don't jump to conclusions by labeling the person as "uncooperative" or "passive aggressive," either in your mind or to their face, which will likely elicit a defensive response or, worse, an irreparable depletion of trust.

As a family leader, it's important for you to keep in mind that people communicate in different ways. Some are outspoken, while others are more introspective and careful. Some family members may not have the words for what they are feeling or are carefully considering what they will say next, not wanting to say something they will have a hard time taking back. In these instances, it may be best for you to step away, letting the person know you want to help them and that when they're ready to speak, you will be ready to listen.

As an elephant herder, it's also important for you to understand that people get stuck in the stories they choose to tell themselves. The longer they've told themselves the story, the more stuck they get. Over a lifetime, people can end up creating neuro-highways for their anger and frustration and a dirt road for a happier version of the same story. In one situation, I watched an entire family system repeatedly bend over backward to try to make one sixty-plus-year-old elephant at the table happy. After having many conversations with this individual, I asked what brought them happiness. There was no answer, only a blank stare. When I expanded on the question, asking, "What fills your heart with so much happiness it brings tears to your eyes?" the person's response was "I don't understand. What do you mean?" To illustrate, I shared an example of my own: I was once hiking in the woods on a beautiful day when a lovely butterfly fluttered across my path. To this, the response through tears was "I've never felt happiness." For me, that was an "aha" moment. An entire family enterprise was exhausting its energy trying to help someone be something they had never been in the past and might never be in the future.

Accept family members for who they are, without judgment. Don't waste your time trying to get them to behave in ways you think will be better for them. This is a waste of valuable energy and time. Family members may share similar DNA, but they may all still be quite different from each other. You have your stories, and they have theirs. You can't change how someone else sees or interacts with the world. If a family member brings unnecessary drama into every family enterprise meeting, it is perfectly fine not to invite their voice to the decision-making table. But remember, they are still welcome at the Sunday family dinner table.

As an elephant herder, be particularly careful not to get dragged into someone's problems with another family member. Empathizing with someone doesn't mean agreeing with them. "I hear what you're saying. You sound sad" is very different from "I agree with what you're saying. You have every right to be mad." Also be cognizant of the "anything is possible" people at the table as opposed to the "negative nellies." The first group will move the family enterprise forward, while the latter will hold your enterprise back from reaching its full potential.

With the lengthened lifespans of many business leaders, sometimes dealing with the elephants in the room will need to skip a generation. For instance, sometimes the difficulties, real or perceived, between siblings can't be overcome because they have been willfully ignored for so long. The cousin group, the third generation, may have an easier time working together because they haven't grown up in close proximity. However, good relationships will be difficult if all those cousins heard growing up was negative stories about their aunts and uncles or other branches of the family. That kind of poisoning can go on for generations, but there is a simple solution: Don't talk negatively about the family business or relatives in front of young members of the upcoming generations.

One final comment: As an elephant herder, you might actually be the elephant in the room. You may not have caused any problems directly, but if you are the family leader, there could be a power imbalance between you and other family members. This power imbalance could explain why figuring out a particular problem has been so difficult: Family members may be more fearful of calling you out. Situations like this will test your success as an effective leader. You need to be aware of the potential for this dynamic and to approach each person you believe is an elephant with deep, respectful listening, and with extra kindness, compassion and empathy. If there is still no resolution, it might be time to seek assistance through an outside professional like a conflict resolution coach or a family therapist.

Role of the Elephant

Are you an elephant? If you believe that you may be the elephant in the room, ask yourself a serious question: Are you acting as a truth teller or a troublemaker? If you're a truth teller, pace your truth-telling to avoid becoming known as a crankypants, a complainer or a difficult family member. Be aware of the impact you're having as well. Too much truth-telling may overwhelm your fellow family members. If you focus mainly on pointing out flaws in decisions or are the consistently negative voice at the table, you might eventually find yourself being rejected or ignored by the other family members.

If something from the past is bothering you, an unresolved issue stemming from an old story that may have become an undiscussable topic, you have three options—and you get to choose which one you take. You can choose to drag that old story everywhere you go for the rest of your life, though decades later you may find yourself aching from a lifetime of carrying it around. You can choose to let go of the story that isn't working for you, to walk away from it and never look back. Or you can choose to discuss the undiscussable, in a facilitated session if necessary, in order to find a way through the old story that is holding you back. Remember, no one is forcing you to keep carrying around that old story—that's entirely your choice.

You gain great power over your life when you see the value in looking forward as opposed to peering over your shoulder to keep a close eye on the past. The work of the successful multi-generational family enterprise is forward-looking; harping on negative old stories is focusing energy in the wrong direction. Letting go of the stories you've chosen to tell yourself is hard, but it will give you the freedom to choose new stories, stories in which you get to redefine who you are today and who you want to be in the future.

Besides, there is a good chance the story you've been telling yourself isn't real. Many of life's difficulties boil down to the way we approach or avoid our problems. In the words of Daniel Kahneman, a noted Israeli-American psychologist and behavioral economist, "The mind sees what it wants to see." Researchers have found that the mind has a way of fooling us based on our biases. For instance, several different people may witness an accident involving a car and a motorcycle and all report a different version of events. Those who have a bias against motorcyclists are more likely to see the motorcyclist as being at fault and those who have a bias against car drivers are more likely to see the car driver as being at fault. And yet, many people get stuck in their version of a story, choosing to make negative assumptions. (Is it really true that elderly family members on a grueling long-distance drive to the funeral of a loved one didn't drive several additional hours out of their way to visit you because they don't love you?)

However, while you might feel more comfortable hanging on to your old stories, even if they make you miserable, there comes a time when you have to ask yourself, "How are these working for me?" Taking responsibility for your choices puts you in control of your life, allowing you to make changes and opening the door to possibility.

Across generations, there may be legacy decisions that are causing resentments in the present. Try to deal with these resentments as soon as they are identified. In a phrase often attributed to Nelson Mandela, "Resentment is like drinking poison and hoping to kill your enemy." Resentment and blame are toxic, and they'll get in the way of your family's multigenerational shared vision.

Your life won't get better by chance; it will only get better by change. You can't change other people, so you have to do the hardest work of all and change yourself, including the stories you choose to tell yourself. And here is the cherry on top: When you change, the people sitting across from you will sometimes change too.

Timing Is Everything

If there's recently been a traumatic event in your family, like the sudden death of a family leader, this is not the time to tackle the elephant in the room. Nor is it the time to approach the family member business board for a sudden pay raise or to quickly move your things into the deceased family leader's office. (I really wish I'd made these scenarios up!) This is the time to give yourself and your family space to grieve, keeping in mind that everyone grieves in different ways. Time is needed for the emotional turmoil to subside and for another family unifier to emerge. It's very important to respect this time period as the family system adjusts to its new family leader.

Where the family business is concerned, it's best not to make any major business decisions during this period but rather to mark the passing of the beloved family leader in a way that genuinely reflects them.

IN SUM, YOU HAVE much to gain by addressing the elephant in the room, including increasing the likelihood that your family enterprise will be successful across multiple generations. You have various potential options for working with the elephant in the room, but skirting the issue is not one of them. Dealing with the elephant in the room is a central, unavoidable role of leadership. The key is to address it as soon as possible. You will find that it is easier to handle elephants now, rather than waiting until they morph into alligators. Releasing the elephant in the room provides the space for fresh air and positive productive energy to flow back into the family enterprise and along with it the ability and opportunity for the family to strengthen its resolve to successfully pursue the now increasingly possible shared multigenerational journey.

8

FAMILY BUSINESS
ADVISORY BOARDS

THERE ARE two main reasons for establishing a family business advisory board: to access alternative ideas and expertise, and to develop the skill of working with qualified individuals who have different perspectives. Based on both my personal experience and my professional work with family enterprises, I believe a family business advisory board, especially one that includes independent members, is a key organizational tool in achieving long-term success.

During the make-or-break fast-paced start-up years in a business, decision-making is often straightforward, with a decision-making structure composed of only one person: the business builder. Making decisions this way allows the new business to react, respond and adapt quickly. Entrepreneurial business builders who have had the vision, perseverance and flexibility to succeed, against all odds, are understandably concerned that working with an advisory board could hold them back. Additionally, business leaders may feel uneasy about the idea of developing formal processes. After all, why would they want to set up time-consuming structures that require them to defend their decisions in what has to date been a successful solo-run business?

The language we use can also play a role in how we feel or react in such circumstances. It can take something that isn't a hassle and make it sound like one—like the term "business advisory board." When some leaders hear that term they think of a board of directors. Boards of directors can strike fear in the hearts of entrepreneurs, because often they represent a formally organized legal body, with rules and regulations that give the directors decision-making authority. In other words, business leaders may worry these entities have the potential to gum up the very flexibility and adaptability that allowed their businesses to be successful in the first place.

However, a business advisory board is meant to be something far less rigid than a formal board of directors. The advisory board usually begins at the sole discretion of the business builder to provide ideas and expertise related to an identified need, say family business transition planning. The business builder might start with a list of points on which they would like outside expertise and then search for the individuals who are the best fit to provide such expertise. There are no rules and regulations or set roles and responsibilities for an advisory board; the board is there to meet the business leader's needs. And as the name implies, an advisory board is about advising, not directing. Unlike a board of directors, an advisory board does not have a vote in decision-making. That remains in the hands of the business leader.

A better name for "advisory board" might be something like "think tank," "idea group" or "forum for solutions," conjuring a space for some real creative thinking. These names make the group sound more like one that is focused on the needs of your business in the pursuit of options and possibility as opposed to an added rigid complicated layer of structure to an already successful business. The goal is to tap experienced people independent of your business for help with what your business needs, and then to discover how comfortable you are incorporating outside perspectives from qualified individuals into your decision-making process.

As your business grows and matures, you'll begin thinking about issues typically outside of your day-to-day operations that need addressing in order for your business to continue to flourish. The challenge is to not ignore these issues but to meet them head-on. Make a list, beginning anywhere, and start knocking the issues off one by one. This is where an enterprise think tank/advisory board can be of assistance. Ignoring issues, like the eventual transition of your business to new management and ownership, especially as you grow older, will create insecurity, unnecessary confusion and unmanaged expectations in the upcoming generation, which in turn can undermine trust and unity.

If you are new to working with people whose ideas are different from yours, there are other ways to try it out before establishing an advisory board. For instance, I've worked with family business leaders who belong to TEC (The Executive Committee International) and other independent leadership groups. These are groups of leaders in non-competing businesses at various stages of business growth who typically meet one day a month with a knowledgeable, experienced business facilitator to work through various questions and solutions, similar to the work of an advisory board.

One advantage of the independent peer groups I've met with is that because the same people have gathered for one day a month for several years, significant trust has built up among members, allowing for candid, unfiltered conversations. It can be challenging, however, to find a peer group that is the right fit for you and has space for new members.

Once you're comfortable working with input from quality independent voices, you're ready to custom-build an advisory board, idea generator or forum for solutions that is 100% focused on your business. In this case, you get to hand-select individuals you already know and trust, choosing people who have the specific skills to meet the needs of your business. You can change the voices at the table whenever change is needed, too, because advisory board members are not legal employees. An advisory board typically meets several times a year, say quarterly, and a small fee is usually paid to advisory board members. I emphasize small, because these are not public companies with substantial directors' fees due to their required legal fiduciary decision-making responsibilities. Advisory board members serve as a way of giving back, by sharing their knowledge, expertise and insights, and supporting the true engines of our economies: those who have defied the odds to create a successful family business.

Finding these candidates is easier than you might think. Business leaders who have built a significant business over a career seem to have no problem finding the right people to sit on their advisory boards. They might not know the individuals personally, at least initially, but when they put the request out through their networks the most remarkable people come to light. In fact, there are many highly experienced, recently retired individuals who are a wealth of information and wisdom.

Start small with the topics covered in your advisory board meetings to see if a group like this works for you. Addressing some of the basics will help you pinpoint where the group could be most useful. By building up slowly, allowing you to gain an appreciation for and confidence in this group, you will discover the many benefits an advisory board can bring to a robust multigenerational family enterprise. For instance, as your business shifts from survival start-up mode to robust growing business, advisory board members can offer input on matters like CEO evaluation, strategic planning, financial analysis (including cash-flow management), key management assessment and other matters unique to a family enterprise. While sought for their specific skills and experience, these advisory board members can also become role models for the upcoming generation. They usually have strong skills to facilitate group cohesion and collaborative board experiences, and they can assist in transparent communication with younger family members, which strengthens trust and unity within the family enterprise.

As you build your advisory board, be aware of the difference between independent and non-independent advisory board members. The role of the independent member is not always the most comfortable one, yet independent members are most valuable to the organization when they are informed and knowledgeable, candidly share their opinions, and weigh in on tough, risky decisions. Some family business advisory boards also include family members, the family business's lawyer and/ or the business's external professional accountant, none of whom are independent. While it is fine to have these people at the table, be cognizant that family members may have biases, especially family member shareholders who are active in the family business. As for the professionals, while they will have insights into the nuances behind operations as they relate to legal and accounting matters, they may also be reluctant to question ideas on the table if that could result in their losing a valuable client.

Independent advisory board members bring two perspectives—advisory and fiduciary—to their work. As advisors, their role is to offer their best advice while recognizing it is the owner's decision whether or not to take it. In their fiduciary role, they have a duty to "do the right thing for all": shareholders, management, employees, etc. Over time, an advisory board member will understand it is time to move on if their advice is constantly ignored. If they believe actions are inappropriately affecting the stakeholders, I believe they are obligated to resign if action isn't taken. So, if you find your advisory board members don't stick around for very long, consider investigating if there is a problem.

Advisory board members should understand what is expected of them prior to joining the board, with a core expectation not only to attend meetings but to be prepared for them and to participate in them. If the board is small—for instance, just the family business leader and a handful of advisory board members—meetings can remain flexible and somewhat informal. As with family meetings, advisory board meeting dates are best set in advance, to respect everyone's schedules, and an agenda should be sent out in good time before the meeting, along with any applicable documents or supporting information.

After thirty-plus years of board experience, I have encountered something new in recent years that is very useful. This is the process of onboarding, which allows new advisory board members to add value as soon as possible. One organization I joined had an "orientation book" that was developed to educate new board members about the organization and the board. The package included a description of the business, the board's bylaws and purpose, bios of the other board members and key management, the directors and officers insurance policy, a list of acronyms used in the organization, and the minutes from one year's worth of meetings. The various business documents in the package included the strategic plan, retirement and transition plans, an organization chart, corporate financials (consolidated for five years, plus one year of detailed financial statements) and useful market information. This isn't an exhaustive list of documents to include in an onboarding package but it worked well for this organization, and it certainly prepared me well for my first meeting. Something similar regarding the operations of your business and the industry it's in, the business's long-term plans, the key players and the role of family will greatly enhance the effectiveness of your advisory board.

Sometimes, advisory board members feel underutilized. If you've sat on a for-profit or not-for-profit board of any kind, you might have experienced this feeling. These are situations in which the CEO effectively runs the meetings, with the chair's role being solely that of calling the meeting to order and adjourning the meeting at the end. In this scenario, very competent, knowledgeable board members sit in silence through the CEO's lengthy presentation, with no solicitation for input based on their independent thoughts. The only questions that arise are from the CEO, who asks the board questions the CEO already knows the answer to.

In a situation like this, the advisory board becomes increasingly ineffectual, and when the company hits a rough spot, as it inevitably will, the advisory board suddenly realizes they aren't on top of the bigger issues. They didn't ask questions about basic assumptions underlying the business or the decisions being made. By that time, it's too late. Something that could have been foreseen and addressed in a thoughtful, proactive way, like a transition in leadership to the upcoming generation, instead happens in a disruptive, reactive way, which has the potential to destabilize the family enterprise.

To avoid this all-too-common problem, there are some simple steps that you, as a family business leader, can take. These include encouraging the independent directors to meet separately to brainstorm about topics they might want to have addressed; leaving time at the end of meetings, without management present, to flesh out ideas that may have come to light during the meeting or to prepare for the next meeting; and meeting individually with each independent director once a year to question them specifically about their two or three top concerns for your family business. The benefits of ensuring ongoing commitment from advisory board members through these three strategies will far outweigh the comparatively small time investment on your part.

Inviting the Second Generation

A smooth-running, effective advisory board is one of the best arenas in which to educate the upcoming generation. Inviting upcoming generation family members who have earned a voice, or are clearly working toward earning a voice, to attend advisory board meetings can be an effective way for them to learn about the business and their future potential roles and responsibilities. In the early years of the second generation attending advisory board meetings, the business builder will often still be the final decision maker. By attending these meetings, the second generation will learn first-hand how the business leader incorporates the ideas of other qualified individuals to make the best decision possible.

Having family meetings at this stage will give second-generation members an opportunity to practice what they are learning at the advisory board meetings: how to incorporate different points of view when making a decision. This will be important as they learn in later years to make joint, consensus-driven decisions.

Beyond addressing the specific needs of your family business, a carefully selected advisory board can also provide the second generation with access to:

· Respected, smart people who share an interest in your family business.
· Role-modeling of useful and effective give-and-take in meetings.
· Helpful thinking on key issues.
· Objective, knowledgeable people to draw on in the case of a sudden death or disability in key leadership.

· Objectivity in conflicts of interest.
· Advocates for active and non-active shareholders.
· Education to strengthen knowledge in the shareholder base.
· Neutrality around policies like family member employment
  and compensation.
· Role-modeling of interactions that feature honesty, clarity,
  transparency and appreciation for different perspectives.

From a timing perspective, if you have not already done
so, this is the point at which to establish a policy for earning a
voice on the advisory board. As previously discussed, once this
policy is created and clearly articulated, share it with your second generation as soon as possible, explaining that it exists to
ensure that quality voices are shared at advisory board meetings because quality voices provide quality input into decisions
that need to be made.

With the second generation involved and you, as the business builder and leader, gaining confidence in the benefits of
an advisory board, your list of topics for meetings could well
expand. Additional topics might include how to:

· Organize upcoming generation family members who are
  active and non-active in the family business.
· Establish parameters for recruiting and selecting future
  independent advisory board members.
· Develop a shareholder redemption policy.
· Facilitate input and communication between leadership in
  the family, family business ownership, family business
  management and upcoming generations of family members.
· Ensure that the business has a strategic plan that aligns with
  ownership's shared values and vision.
· Ensure that there is a process in place to groom upcoming
  leaders of the family, family business ownership and family
  business management.

Working through these kinds of issues with the independent advisory board members and members of the upcoming generation provides fertile ground to cover in preparing upcoming generations of owners.

As for the mechanics of advisory board meetings, once you have second-generation members at the table, continue to prepare an agenda in advance, but also be sure to circulate full minutes after each meeting. These minutes provide a terrific educational record for future generations by capturing the who, when, where, why, how and what of the decisions that were made. The worst-case scenario I've seen was in a family business that had never created minutes for meetings. It was told by a second-generation family member who worked in the business that a highly contentious, significant capital expenditure that would benefit his department had been approved by the recently deceased family leader. When the family questioned the details of the approval, the member presented, purportedly from the meeting in question, minutes: a five-line blurb approving the capital expenditure. Of course, this person's action significantly depleted the trust of the other family members. Please, please produce accurate minutes that are circulated to and approved by all advisory board members who attended the meeting and then enter these minutes into the records of your family business.

Finally, every meeting runs better when the person leading it actively encourages the input of all those attending. An effective meeting leader uses gentle communication skills and listens with an open heart and mind. In the early years, the business leader often leads the advisory board, finding the job quite easy. When second-generation family members become involved, the role of the meeting leader will become more important, as family members learn to work together at the advisory board table rather than the dinner table. The meeting leader may need additional patience at first, but if the family members at the advisory board meetings have earned a voice—which includes being reasonable people—the meetings will soon flow easily, becoming a normal and natural part of the family enterprise.

Inviting the Third Generation

By the time third-generation members are old enough to earn a voice on the family business advisory board, there may well be too many people for an efficient decision-making group. Consider creating a policy regarding the size of the advisory board, since eventually there will be too many family members for them all to have a seat on the board at the same time. Independent advisory board members are also less likely to agree to serve on a board with a dozen or more family members, from a fear that meetings could end up in "analysis paralysis" because of too many earned voices at the table.

By the third generation, the advisory board will be considering the needs not only of the family business but also of the family enterprise. That means the make-up of the board may change. Some advisory boards are there to advise management; others are there to protect family shareholders not active in the family business. Some advisory board members have a broad range of skills and expertise; others are more narrowly focused. An active family member shareholder owner/manager, for instance, might want a group of board members who are in agreement with their strategy and can help them achieve their goals, asking them questions but ultimately supporting them. Conversely, non-active family member shareholders may want an advisory board group composed of individuals who are critical and vigorously challenge the active family shareholder group, who believe in the family's shared values and vision and will represent the non-active family shareholders' best interests.

Third and future generations will need to understand the three systems that exist in a family enterprise—the family, family business ownership and family business management—and that it is critical for family matters not to spill over into the family business, and vice versa. As noted, in the early start-up stages, it's not typical for a family business builder and leader to make a distinction among these three systems. However, it is useful for third and future generations to think this way, wrapping their minds around possible roles, responsibilities and opportunities in each of the three systems.

From the two original groups, the family meeting group and the family business advisory board, families at the third-generation stage evolve to create a third body, the ownership group, thereby removing ownership discussions from both family meetings and family business advisory board meetings. At this point, all three systems are independently represented in the family enterprise framework: the family (Family Council), family business ownership (Owners' Council) and family business management (Family Business Advisory Board).

Additionally, because ownership in the business has often expanded from the original business builder to possibly quite an unwieldy number of family members at this stage, families will want to change the way decisions are made, with the Family Council, Owners' Council and Family Business Advisory Board becoming separate decision-making bodies. The Family Council has decision-making authority over matters relating to family members and the family as a whole; the Owners' Council sets the shared values and vision of the family business in conjunction with the family's own shared values and vision; and the Family Business Advisory Board ensures that management is setting a course and working toward objectives that align with the directives from the Owners' Council.

Additionally, by the third generation and beyond, it's possible that a large number of family members will have earned a voice to serve on the councils and/or boards of the family enterprise. Since there may well be too many people for everyone to serve at once, it's useful for the third generation to review and expand the policy on earning a voice, adding mechanisms for family members who've earned a voice to be elected to the available seats in the different decision-making groups.

IN SUMMARY, don't establish a business advisory board before you're ready for one. Put the board in place once you're clear it would help you to have input from other qualified independent voices as your business grows. As with building a business, there is no right way to build an advisory board, but my suggestion is to start small. By beginning with a few trusted and respected individuals, you'll discover that the benefits of an advisory board extend beyond commonly encountered business topics into topics that you might have never considered on your own. With an increased number of family members in later generations, creating a strong family enterprise framework that includes a Family Council, an Owners' Council and a Family Business Advisory Board positions your family and your family business to flourish for generations to come. In the end, you're not alone anymore.

9

YOUR FAMILY OFFICE

Co-authored with Paul K. Hamilton

GENERALLY SPEAKING, the term "Family Office" is used to describe how a family organizes itself when it has amassed a certain amount of personal financial wealth, perhaps through the sale of a business or by having accumulated wealth from the business. In our work with Family Offices and family office members from around the globe, it became clear to us that there is no one clear definition of a Family Office. Every Family Office is unique to the family it serves. What follows is an overview of Family Offices, including the four stages commonly encountered when establishing a Family Office.

There is the idea, largely encouraged by the media, that a Family Office is something created by only the wealthiest families in the world. Billionaire brothers Charles and David Koch, for instance, established 1888 Management to manage a small portion of their estimated US$86 billion in combined net worth. However, similar to an iceberg, for every Family Office in the public eye, such as Oprah Winfrey's OW Management, there are many more that are intentionally private, hidden just below the surface of the media's radar. With significant financial wealth to manage, the scope and structure of Family Offices range from a family leader orchestrating operations from their home, outsourcing the services required, to a stand-alone fully integrated legal operational entity.

The common reason for establishing a Family Office is to create a structure through which significant family wealth can be managed. There are other reasons for establishing a Family Office, however, including the desire to preserve family wealth by increasing wealth-management efficiencies by consolidating all the family's assets under one operational umbrella. Additionally, many families use the Family Office structure as a way to deal with family conflicts and to ensure that financial wealth is appropriately transitioned to future generations.

So, where to start? An important thing to know is that establishing a Family Office typically occurs over a two-to-five-year period. The first two stages are primarily concerned with money management, or quantitative issues. The last two stages also include thinking and planning regarding the family itself, or qualitative issues.

Stage 1: Financial Freedom

Financial freedom arises for a number of reasons, including having accumulated financial capital over your career or as a result of selling your business. If it is the latter, the odd question may linger in your mind about whether you made the right decision by selling your robust business, but these concerns will disappear once the sale proceeds are received and the deal is done, and will be quickly replaced by a newfound sense of financial freedom. However, no matter how your financial freedom comes about, some fun spending might be the first action you take, perhaps an overdue family vacation or some previously put-off home renovations. Go ahead and enjoy your fun spending. You earned it.

Becoming a successful steward of significant liquid capital can be a learning process. Generally, the managing of this financial wealth can be looked at as having three parts. Part one is a time of preparation and planning for the investment and lifestyle decisions you will be making. Part two is a time for action, putting the money to work. Part three is defined by monitoring your annual progress toward the goals you have set and sharing your wealth with your family and community.

"But what about managing the money?" you ask. Entrepreneurs can have a difficult time becoming investors; likewise, good investors are not necessarily good entrepreneurs. Each activity requires a completely different skill set. Wealth creation often occurs through concentrated business building and wealth preservation, and growth occurs through more diversification. An entrepreneur's instinct can be to over-concentrate on business building and in the process take unwarranted risks.

Entrepreneurs tend to be active investors. They have a need to feel in control of their investments, often becoming highly involved in the investment process. By being actively involved and feeling in control, these investors feel they are reducing risk. Some have difficulty delegating decisions to others, which can lead to discontent. As a result, an entrepreneur will wrestle with the role of being an active or a passive investor. The need to feel in control of one's investments will always be there, as it should be. However, the general advice here is to start by investing extremely conservatively rather than making the mistake of investing in risky ventures.

During this first stage, the priorities with regard to money management are liquidity, preservation of capital and safety of capital. This means parking your accumulating excess capital and/or significant proceeds at a fiscally sound financial institution in cash and cash equivalents. Financial institutions have been known to fail, so be certain you understand the institution's balance sheets, who regulates them and how strictly they are regulated. When you're looking for a financial institution in which to deposit significant funds, it makes sense to shop around for the best rates, but be careful not to jeopardize the safety of your capital. In other words, knowing that risk and return go hand in hand, be sure that you are comfortable with the level of risk you're taking if you decide to leave your significant funds in a financial institution that offers higher deposit interest rates but has a riskier financial institution profile.

Further, ensure that the financial professionals you work with and the financial institution itself are insured, reputable and highly regulated. For instance, ask questions about the role of compliance and the specific steps the firm will take to ensure your money is invested in the way you have expressly agreed to.

Stage 2: Financial Investment Management

As you continue to decompress from the years spent building your business, followed by the physical and emotional process if you sold it, your sharp business mind will be aware that leaving your funds in cash and cash equivalent accounts over the long term is a sure way to erode your financial legacy when the interest earned on cash is less than inflation. In addition to being mindful of liquidity, preservation and the safety of your capital, a common next step is to begin to invest in the financial markets to add an element of growth and diversity, which is accompanied by risk, to the management of your funds.

Transitioning from cash and cash equivalent investments to equity and fixed income investments is a standard way to access growth for your capital. As a general proposition, families who have taken substantial risks in building their businesses and are seeking growth for their capital over the long term like to keep risk low at this early stage while they continue to get more comfortable in thinking about the future, including deciding on allocating their capital between direct investments in other businesses or indirectly through the financial markets.

A major change many families face is going from owning a private business to owning publicly traded securities, whose prices change every day. Actually, when you owned your family business, the price of that business also changed from day to day. Had you tried to sell it on different days, you would likely have received different offers, because your business was valued based on market inputs such as interest rates and the market price of similar companies, which change daily. You, of course, didn't see these changes reflected on your account statements in the way you do when you own publicly traded securities, and that difference is paramount—seeing the value of your assets change every day can be an emotional roller coaster.

In order to manage these emotions, it is key that you understand what you are investing in. Choosing shares and bonds of solid businesses that are profitable, growing steadily and relatively simple to understand is a good place to start. There is often the temptation to invest in assets that offer the highest possible return, but this usually comes with equally high risk and a more aggressive roller coaster ride. Frankly, at this stage, most families want to keep their risk low.

There are many statistical measurements of risk and volatility. As an example, one way of measuring risk is through standard deviation, which is simply a measure of how much a stock or bond's price moves around from day to day—its volatility. Standard deviation is by no means a perfect measure (for instance, a stock that moves up 50% will have the same standard deviation as one that moves down 50%), but it is something to watch, particularly at this early stage. The higher the standard deviation of your portfolio, the harder it will be to manage your emotions. That's important, since this situation can translate into families selling stocks and bonds at their lows and buying them back at their highs—the opposite of what you're aiming for. The point here is that you will have to embrace the idea that investments will continually change in value.

Paying attention to where and when to invest and to the volatility of your investments is also important in these early years because, as other investment opportunities present themselves, you don't want to be forced to sell a portion of your portfolio at a market low. Stocks that move around less generally don't fall as much, so if you have to sell to invest in something else, the cost to you is not as great.

As family leader, you need to remain informed about the overall risk level of your investments. Specifically, you need to understand the distinction between illiquid and liquid investments and the different levels of risk associated with them. For instance, the business you just sold was an illiquid investment, in that while it represented a monetary value, you couldn't easily access this theoretical pool of cash; hence the expression "asset rich, cash poor." Investments in stock markets are liquid, and they allow for the sale of an investment with quite literally the push of a button.

Preserving your capital while moving deeper into the financial markets means fully understanding the nature of individual stocks, investment funds and investment products. We will stop here on the nature, purpose and form of investing and the financial markets as they are not the focus of this book. Others write extensively on this subject matter, making this an ideal topic for further study.

Many twenty-first-century financial professionals are talented product promoters and salespeople, who have often been honing their craft for decades. Commonly, they'll tell you about all the benefits but none of the drawbacks of their investment products, assuring you that their product is right for everyone. Another approach professionals may take is to try to sell you on complex investment strategies. Be cautious, though, because complexity often backfires at the worst possible time.

Finally, an added degree of safety is gained through diversifying your wealth. Previously, your wealth may have been tied up in your business. In other words, you may have had all your eggs in one basket. Accessing the financial markets allows you to reduce your overall risk by diversifying, spreading your investments across industries, continents and asset classes— or by putting your eggs in many different baskets. Over time, entrepreneurs come to welcome the benefits of diversification through a more balanced portfolio.

While this second stage can seem daunting, and undoubtedly requires careful thought, here are a few key points to help you navigate your way through it:

1) Manage your risk carefully, recognizing that your primary goal is to first preserve and then grow your capital gradually over time.

2) Do careful research on investment solutions.

3) Be cognizant that some investment professionals are promoters and/or salespeople who receive incentives for selling you their products.

4) Avoid too much complexity early on.

5) Diversify your portfolio across industries, geography and asset classes (fixed income, equity, etc.).

In around two to five years, entrepreneurs evolve and become more sophisticated investors. They also come to appreciate that they are managing their financial resources not just for themselves but for many constituents, including spouses, children, grandchildren and charitable foundations.

Stage 3: Reflection

As a family business builder, you likely spent a portion of your career reacting to situations beyond your control and answering to a number of stakeholders, such as employees, shareholders and customers. Now you have time for reflection, the wisdom gained from past business experiences and a wonderful opportunity to be the decision maker, proactively designing your Family Office.

With a chance to decompress, adjust to the new routines in your life and understand that your financial capital is being managed to achieve liquidity, preservation of capital, safety of capital and prudent growth, this is also a good time to reflect on the research, which indicates that 70% of families lose control of their financial wealth over each generation, largely due to factors that lie within the family itself: inattention, mismanagement, miscommunication, family feuding and/or foolish expenditures. A way to overcome the failure rate is to follow the approach described in my book *Build Your Family Bank*, which outlines how multigenerational financial investment management families can successfully organize their human and intellectual assets, the family members and all they know, so that they do not lose control of their financial wealth.

Similar to the work described in this book, the Family Bank approach to building your Family Office begins with the articulation of your family's shared values and vision. It then progresses with an honest assessment of all the assets in your family, not only the financial but also the human and intellectual assets, followed by the creation of a Family Office framework (a governance structure) that assists in ensuring the best decisions possible are made by upcoming decision makers in your family and your Family Office. By following an approach like this, you will be able to build a Family Office that addresses not only financial, or quantitative factors, but also family issues, or qualitative factors.

Stage 4: Structuring Your Family Office

As your life transitions and your family evolves, what you want your Family Office to achieve, and thereby the services your Family Office will need to provide, will also evolve. From the humble beginnings of an owner-operated Family Office to a possible stand-alone Family Office, the services you can access range from family bookkeeping services, with the investment management being outsourced, to a full menu of services like:

· In-house investment and/or asset management
· Financial planning
· Insurance plans
· Tax planning
· Risk analysis
· Philanthropy
· Family Office framework
· Education

The common factor is that some kind of investing and/or asset management lies at the core of your Family Office.

When we look at this list, we see quantitative factors, like investment and asset management, financial planning, insurance and tax planning, and risk analysis, and qualitative factors, like Family Office framework and education. We enjoy the logic and predictability of numbers, but we're always curious about the unpredictability, or the human influence, behind qualitative factors. Even with the strongest legal, accounting and financial management structures in place, a family can still lose control of its financial wealth, as noted, for reasons that lie within the family itself. As you settle into the new role of leading your Family Office, consider that running a business aimed at unknown customers can be easy compared to running one that serves you and your family members.

This is where your Family Office framework and education come in. A good Family Office framework allows you to establish policies and structures that ensure the decisions being made support the well-being of both your Family Office and your family members. Education assists in preparing the future generation leaders of your Family Office to continue the legacy of making quality decisions.

As discussed in previous chapters, the strongest policies are those that are largely accepted by family members. Effective policies are based on decisions agreed to by family members, and family members are more likely to agree to these decisions when they understand how the decisions support their well-being and that of your Family Office. Strong, clearly articulated and largely agreed-to Family Office policies, like those described in Chapter 6, aid family harmony because they manage family members' expectations, prepare them for their future roles and responsibilities, and help them avoid many of tomorrow's predictable problems.

Education plays a vital role in the agreed-to decision-making process, because it teaches family members that, as mentioned previously, qualified voices make quality decisions. A common situation is that the family leader has built the business in conjunction with their right-hand person, perhaps a trusted CFO. When the business is sold, the CFO is hired by the family to run the Family Office and invest the family's financial assets. Even when this individual does a terrific job, family members can become dependent on the arrangement, inadvertently robbing family members of many learning opportunities, both financial and qualitative.

For instance, maybe a family member needs to secure a mortgage for their first home purchase. They call the Family Office—done. The CFO handles it. A family member is going through a divorce. They call the Family Office—done. The CFO handles it. Then the family trust is being rewritten, and the CFO needs family member signatures, but only the signing page is sent to the family members. Done. The family members sign, not wanting to question the family leader or the CFO about the full contents of the trust document. If, however, the family member in question had shadowed the CFO when their mortgage was secured, one step toward their financial education would have been taken. If the divorcing family member had independently handled their divorce, one step toward marital maturity and financial education would have been taken. And if family members had been encouraged to read the trust document they were signing and ask questions about it, then one step toward estate planning education would have been taken. The Family Office can be a great educational tool for preparing family members—some of whom will serve as Family Office leaders in the future—to effectively manage advisors, review financial statements and strategically decide how services will be provided.

On the quantitative side, the direction you take in managing your family's financial wealth depends on how much capital you have to manage, what you want to achieve, what your risk tolerance is and where your interests lie. For instance, if you're interested in the real estate market and you have knowledge, expertise and a good track record, perhaps all your Family Office needs is a seasoned real estate manager to manage your property acquisitions. Or, rather than owning the properties directly, families may decide to invest in reputable real estate companies that trade on highly regulated stock exchanges. Other families will pursue a hybrid investment strategy, which combines direct real estate ownership and financial securities ownership.

Many families have great success in forming Family Office investment committees. The investments these committees oversee can vary widely. At one end of the spectrum are committees of sophisticated investors, with members overseeing complex financial investment portfolios managed by experienced investment staff in the Family Office. At the other end are committees with members who may lack financial investment expertise but bring knowledge, advice and insights regarding alternative investments in private businesses or real estate.

The investment committees for large, sophisticated Family Offices will play a different role than will committees for smaller Family Offices. Ultimately, the role that's appropriate for your Family Office investment committee will depend on a number of factors. These include the size of your Family Office and its portfolio, your family's culture and history, the presence or absence of experienced in-house investment staff, the experience and sophistication of other members of the committee, and the financial objectives of your Family Office.

One family we've worked with has a large number of family members who have physical domiciles across the globe. This family has assembled an Advisory Board for their Family Office, whose independent members, along with key family members, include some of the world's leading experts in Family Office framework ("governance"), succession and wealth transition planning, and legal and tax planning. With regard to the qualitative management of the family, they have a small, one-person Family Office situated in one city that focuses on family matters.

The decisions regarding the physical make-up of your Family Office and the associated costs will be similar to the kinds of decisions you made while you were building your successful business. For instance, the operating costs associated with establishing a separate, stand-alone office and employing full-time professional staff can be reasonable when you have $1 billion to manage but may not be cost-effective if you have $25 million to manage. Setting up a "bricks and mortar" Family Office is naturally going to cost more to operate than one in which you outsource management to third-party managers.

You will know best what makes sense both financially and practically.

One exciting option in the twenty-first century is Virtual Family Offices, which allow you to avoid the bricks and mortar question and potential issues with finding and managing appropriately qualified Family Office personnel. The full menu of Family Office services can be outsourced, and that gives you access to the best services in the world.

Another phenomenon we've come across on the global stage is the creation of Multifamily Family Offices (MFOs). A Single-Family Office (SFO) is a Family Office that is set up to serve one family. Some SFOs reach a point where they say, "Hey, we're providing all these services to the many branches of our family; maybe we can defray the cost by charging other families a fee for us to manage their money, while providing them access to our other Family Office services."

But wait! Family Office advisory work is now being vigorously pursued by lawyers, accountants and even banks, so exercise caution. When seeking the expertise of any advisor, be very clear about what you need. In the case of Family Office advisors, be wary of investment advisors who offer nothing more than basic investment management, maybe even then only providing access to products of the firm they work for like mutual funds and other products or advice that only promotes the recommended list of their firm, and yet entice you into opening accounts by calling themselves MFOs. In the case of banks, some employ individuals who may simply have attended a few courses to become "certified" family business advisors and whose "Family Office services" are linked to many different investment advisors. It's impossible to imagine one person providing a quality level of service to the hundreds of different clients that working with more than one investment advisor usually entails.

You will want to find advisors who have real concrete action plans and specific deliverables on not just the quantitative aspects of your Family Office but also the qualitative. Ask questions and dig deep into the specific services they offer when it comes to the qualitative work. You might discover that although an advisor markets their team as an MFO, the team doesn't offer the full range of capabilities and attention that your situation requires.

To sum up, the distinguishing trait of a Family Office is how it organizes itself to address not only quantitative, or financially focused, matters but also qualitative factors, the family itself. In every example we've come across, investing and/or asset management of some kind has been at the heart of the Family Office. But if a Family Office focuses only on the heart muscle, managing the family's financial affairs, and pays no attention to the health of the blood flowing through the heart, the family members and their relationship to the Family Office, then the Family Office may end up serving only the professionals in charge.

10

FAMILY ENTERPRISE ADVISORS

I HAVE INCLUDED this chapter on family enterprise advisors because you and your family may need their services in order to move your family along on your journey. A family enterprise advisor assists with the content—the what—and the process—the how—of families who want to create a successful family enterprise framework, decision-making processes and policies. One of the key ways they do this is by facilitating family meetings, which allow family members to strengthen their levels of trust and communication, prepare the upcoming generation and develop a shared vision.

What should you look for when selecting a family enterprise advisor? A good place to start is with some research on the subject of family enterprises and some of the topics discussed in this book. The bibliography at the end of this book is a curated selection from the copious literature published on the subject. What you'll discover as you start to read is that a family working together doesn't require any highly specialized academic skills. Unlike completing a tax return or establishing a legal structure, there are no hard-and-fast rules when it comes to creating your successful family enterprise. The ideas you come across when doing this research are best used to spark your imagination, because the specific process and outcomes will be unique to your family.

For instance, one academic resource attempts to explain how the three systems in the family enterprise—the family, family business ownership and family business management—interrelate by using a model that looks similar to a chain of DNA. While this model is interesting, in my opinion it unnecessarily complicates the subject. Another academic writer created an overlapping three-circle model, representing the three systems in a family enterprise, to explain why conflicts, or differences of opinion, arise. While this model is elegant, I wish the sources of conflict in a family enterprise were that simple. Dealing with the root causes of conflict takes time, effort, patience and often willingness for people to change their opinions. However, the role that conflict could play in your family enterprise is an idea worth considering.

After you have some research under your belt, you might decide to start looking for a family enterprise advisor. Working from the thirty-thousand-foot level, do the sorts of things you would do in hiring any kind of consultant, such as meeting with them to see if there is any chemistry between you. The purpose of this casual first meeting, which should be attended by the family business leader and anyone else who controls the decisions being made, is to gain an understanding of the family enterprise advisor's process, including fees, the timing of the work and the deliverables you can expect. If you don't click with the potential advisor, that's okay; there are lots more advisors out there. Don't engage someone just because you want it to work or because that person worked well with your good friend's family. Trust is crucial in this process.

When you find an advisor you like, check their references and educational background. This is still a new area of study, with programs and certificates popping up everywhere. All many require is the equivalent of a one-semester university course before the awarding of some kind of "expert" designation, such as Family Business Advisor. Do your vetting here, because if you have a financially successful family business, potential advisors will be drawn to your doorstep.

In some instances, the courses taken by professionals like accountants, lawyers and bankers are really about selling successful families certain kinds of products. Many of these individuals do not actually engage with families by facilitating family meetings, doing the profound work of really listening, exercising intense curiosity or seeking to uncover problems that may stand in the way of your family's multigenerational journey. Instead, they are focused on selling you tax-planning work, trust structures and banking and investment products.

Be wary as well of family enterprise advisors who offer quick checklist solutions. If a family enterprise advisor is keen for you to implement what makes sense to them based on lectures they've attended and a program they've recently completed—or worse, their results with another family—run! Success for your family over multiple generations doesn't lie in prescribed textbook answers but in the probing questions asked by a skilled family enterprise advisor. Helping your family reach a shared vision for current and future generations will take an intense, sustained effort on the part of your advisor. A skilled family enterprise advisor has to spend the time and energy actively listening, asking questions and checking in on answers, and then thinking long and hard about your family and the long-term journey your family wants to embark on.

Furthermore, "I know what's best for you" is a red flag. If they already have all the answers and know what's best for you, it's very likely they will not be listening to you. Just as active listening is critical to strengthening communication and reducing conflict in a family, it is also critical to the work of a family enterprise advisor. Active listening means your advisor has to leave predetermined solutions at the door. A good family enterprise advisor will set aside their own beliefs and judgments in favor of curiosity. You'll know you have the right person when they are asking questions based on where you and your family are taking the conversation, rather than offering a ready-made solution to a yet-to-be-determined problem.

Some advisors sell their services as experts who will come in and create a "governance" (there's that word again) structure and accompanying policies for your family enterprise. This is a quantifiable, actionable product to sell, and after all, successful multigenerational family enterprises need a family enterprise framework and accompanying policies, right? But there's a big problem with that approach. It's frustrating to spend time and money on a smooth-talking family enterprise advisor who imposes structures and rules your family members aren't ready for. The magic of your family enterprise framework, with its accompanying decision-making processes and policies, is not only that you have these things but also that you've gone through a process with your family to create them. Textbook solutions rob you and your family of the most important part of your shared journey. The process of working together will strengthen trust, communication and unity, and help prepare members of your family system for how they'll work together in the future, including when life throws them curveballs.

Because each family business has its own unique culture, be careful about instituting what a family enterprise advisor recommends as "best practices," especially if it changes the ways things are currently done. For instance, one family may consider it acceptable for family members to provide undocumented loans to family members. A family enterprise advisor may not find this is a best practice, but if it works for this family, that's what matters most. In other words, it's the practice that works best for the family that matters most and not what the family enterprise advisor believes is best for the family.

Another scenario to be wary of is a family enterprise advisor who relies on genograms and birth-order research to explain what is happening in your family. Some family members may attempt to justify their behavior by pointing to the family genogram or their birth order. A reputable family enterprise advisor will help family members to understand that they are not products of these forces but instead are products of the stories they choose to tell themselves and that each individual is accountable for their own choices and decisions.

As outlined earlier, to create a successful multigenerational family enterprise, families need to start by exploring their shared values and vision. Because these initial family meetings are so critical, it's important to work with a family enterprise advisor who has facilitation skills and can create an environment in which all family members feel safe to express themselves. Good family enterprise advisors pay close attention not only to what is being said but also to what they see happening at the table. They pay attention to both the big issues and the smallest details. There is quite enough going on for family members at the meeting table without their being distracted by an inattentive or disorganized family meeting facilitator.

It can be a leap of faith for family members to enter into family meetings. Each person at the family meeting table is counting on the family enterprise advisor to have their backs, to hold the space for them. A good advisor will ensure that every voice is heard and every person listened to. This isn't always easy, especially if someone is being unkind or unreasonable, but it is the advisor's job to infuse the meeting with empathy, compassion and genuine curiosity. Every family enterprise deserves an advisor who digs deep and checks their judgments at the door.

Even with all of this care, however, you may feel that one or another family member is being pigeonholed by the advisor. This can happen unintentionally; family enterprise advisors are human beings, and like all humans they have biases. Sometimes an unconscious bias can lead even the most skilled advisor to jump to the wrong conclusion. If this seems to be happening, have a conversation with the advisor about your concerns. If you are not satisfied with the outcome, it might be time to switch advisors.

There's no room for a family enterprise advisor who is condescending or claims to know what is best for your family. A family enterprise advisor's work isn't easy, because no two humans or families are identical. Prescriptive solutions are a lazy advisor's way of failing to recognize the human and intellectual attributes of each family member and the potential for all members to work together toward a shared goal.

Be wary as well of any family enterprise advisor who gives you a specific timeline at the outset. I've learned over the years that until I've worked with a family to help them discover their shared values and vision, and have seen from that what the levels of trust and communication are in the family, I have no idea exactly which steps will be required for them to reach their goals. However, I always make it very clear from the start that I'm not interested in permanent, ongoing work with a family, because the most successful families are the ones who eventually take this work on for themselves.

That all being said, the general progression of this work is the same. As outlined in earlier chapters, initial steps typically include articulating the family's shared values and vision; creating a family meeting code of conduct; having an ownership discussion and perhaps even creating an ownership pledge; facilitating a fundamental understanding of the family enterprise framework; establishing accompanying decision-making processes; and creating core policies related to earning a voice, defining family, employment of family members, compensation, shareholder agreements and pre-determination agreements. In a family where all members are both shareholders and active in the family business, and the family has high trust and strong communication skills, these topics can be moved through quite quickly. In another situation, where trust is high and communication is strong but family business knowledge is low—because upcoming generation family members are all working independently of the family, for instance—then extra time and additional meetings may be needed for shared learning purposes.

Family enterprise advisors must also be very careful about getting too close to family members. A family's trust in their advisor is as important as trust within the family group. The family enterprise advisor needs to maintain space for everyone to be their best. Getting too close to individual members can lead to the family enterprise advisor losing objectivity and, even worse, losing the ability to be seen by all family members as supporting the collective good.

As you undertake the journey of building a multigenerational family enterprise, success won't be found in the work done by a family enterprise advisor; it will be found in the work your family does for itself. Your family enterprise will flourish only when your family rolls up its sleeves and members sit down as a group to find answers together. The main things a good family enterprise advisor will carry away from working alongside your family are gratitude for your trust and admiration for your family for entering into this process, no matter where it leads.

CONCLUSION:
Embarking on the Journey

THIS IS AN EXCITING journey you are embarking on, one available to you because of a lifetime of hard work and the acumen and calculated risk it takes to create a thriving family business. Having read this book, you are now armed with the core insights and strategies that will assist you in building a successful multigenerational family enterprise.

As discussed, this journey begins with the articulation of your family's shared values, followed by the creation of your shared vision: what your family collectively wants to achieve. Your shared values and vision may sound like soft topics, but they provide the foundation for a large number of family members to make the best decisions possible. They remind family members about what's important to them. Having been through this process with my own family and with families whose meetings I've facilitated, I'm inspired time and again by people's willingness to share with one another their heartfelt pride in what makes their family special. Your shared values and vision will also fuel the commitment and perseverance necessary for your family to pursue its long-term goal of becoming a successful multigenerational family enterprise.

A multigenerational family generates enormous value for themselves and the future of the family when they work together to earn their own success. Families who choose to work together also discover ways to maintain harmony and unity when the journey presents problems they could never have anticipated. On a seven-generation journey, only the unexpected can be expected without fail.

The journey of every family and family business is unique, but unique doesn't mean impossible. Oftentimes it only means that time is needed for the required elements of your successful multigenerational family enterprise to evolve in their own way. The work put in by you and your family to create a successful multigenerational family enterprise is led by curiosity and followed up with desire and adaptability. Many families discover it can be fun to explore what might be possible.

After all your hard work, now is a good time to sit back, relax a little and enjoy the process. Take a well-earned break as you allow the upcoming generation of family members who have earned, or are clearly earning, a voice to bring their full creative selves to the table. By giving these individuals more latitude, you just might find yourself wonderfully surprised.

I have a quote on my desk that was framed by one of my sons: "Shoot for the moon. Even if you miss, you'll land among the stars." It's a leap of faith for families to leave behind old habits and ways of doing things to head toward the unknown. By taking this journey, you and your family will discover together how far your family enterprise might travel. Whether it's the moon or the stars or somewhere in between, families who embark on this journey will earn the admiration and profound respect of current and future generations.

BIBLIOGRAPHY

ORTUNATELY FOR families and their businesses, access to information about successful multigenerational family businesses in the twenty-first century is almost limitless. Warren Buffett is quoted as saying, "Read 500 pages like this every day. That's how knowledge works. It builds up like compound interest." The content in this book has been distilled from a significant body of this compound interest, including my independent substantive research of multigenerational family businesses and family enterprises from multiple sources ranging from written texts; conferences, talks and podcasts; and interactions with peer-to-peer family enterprise organizations.

On the written front, this book is a companion to my first book, *Build Your Family Bank: A Winning Vision for Multigenerational Wealth*. In *Build Your Family Bank*, I explain how to create your own Family Bank, beginning with a solid foundation of your family's shared values and vision, and how you can assess all of your family's assets—human, intellectual and financial— and prepare succeeding generations to steward those assets successfully. With respect to financial assets, *Build Your Family Bank* focused on family enterprises that were managing financial wealth generated from the sale of a family business or accumulated outside the family business. While this book has the same foundational philosophy as *Build Your Family Bank*, its focus is on one specific kind of financial asset in a family enterprise: the family business and its relationship with the family.

For information on family businesses and enterprises, two of my favorite and recommended authors are Professors John L. Ward and Craig E. Aronoff, who have both individually and collaboratively published extensively. Aronoff is co-founder, principal consultant and chairman of the board of the Family Business Consulting Group, Inc., headquartered out of Chicago, Illinois, and the founder of the Cox Family Enterprise Center and current professor emeritus at Kennesaw State University. He invented and implemented the membership-based, professional service provider–sponsored Family Business Forum, which has served as a model of family business education for universities worldwide. John L. Ward is co-founder of the Family Business Consulting Group, Inc. He is a clinical professor at the Kellogg School of Management and teaches strategic management, business leadership and family enterprise continuity. While there are many other excellent writers in this subject area, Aronoff's and Ward's combined body of work is extensive and insightful, and provides solid information for family enterprises and family businesses that want to succeed across the generations.

Other sources of unbiased insightful information in the twenty-first century include peer-to-peer groups, like Campden Wealth, London, UK, which is an independent family-owned business providing unrivaled knowledge, intelligence and connectivity for family businesses around the world. It brings together family members, including family business leaders, to share and learn from one another's inspired multi-generational family enterprise success stories. Additionally, extensive online resources give us unparalleled access to quality articles specifically about family business and family enterprise. For instance, the Family Business Consulting Group, co-founded by Aronoff and Ward, which, along with numerous

other experts in the field of family businesses and family
enterprises, provides a substantial online database of useful
information. Other excellent sources of information, especially
for those who may be pressed for reading time but do have listening time available, are audiobooks and podcasts like The
Jordan Harbinger Show, which are a growing source of informed
curated quality content.

GENERAL RESOURCES

Aronoff, Craig E. *Letting Go: Preparing Yourself to Relinquish Control
of the Family Business.* New York: Palgrave Macmillan, 2011.

Aronoff, Craig E., Joseph H. Astrachan, Drew S. Mendozza, and John
L. Ward. *Making Sibling Teams Work: The Next Generation.* New York;
Palgrave Macmillan, 2011.

Aronoff, Craig E., Joseph H. Astrachan, and John L. Ward. *Developing
Family Business Policies: Your Guide to the Future.* New York: Palgrave
Macmillan, 2010.

Aronoff, Craig E., and Otis W. Baskin. *Effective Leadership in the Family
Business.* New York: Palgrave Macmillan, 2011.

Aronoff, Craig E., Stephen L. McClure, and John L. Ward. *Family Business Compensation.* New York: Palgrave Macmillan, 2011.

———. *Family Business Ownership: How to Be An Effective Shareholder.* New
York: Palgrave Macmillan, 2011.

———. *Family Business Succession: The Final Test of Greatness.* New York:
Palgrave Macmillan, 2011.

Aronoff, Craig E., and John L. Ward. *Family Business Governance:
Maximizing Family and Business Potential.* New York: Palgrave
Macmillan, 2010.

———. *Family Business Values: How to Assure a Legacy of Continuity and
Success.* New York: Palgrave Macmillan, 2011.

———. *Family Meetings: How to Build a Stronger Family and a Stronger
Business.* New York: Palgrave Macmillan, 2010.

———. *From Siblings to Cousins: Prospering in the Third Generation and
Beyond.* New York: Palgrave Macmillan, 2011.

———. *How to Choose and Use Advisors: Getting the Best Professional Family
Business Advice.* New York: Palgrave Macmillan, 2010.

———. *Make Change Your Family Business Tradition.* New York: Palgrave
Macmillan, 2011.

———. *More than Family: Non-Family Executives in the Family Business*. New York: Palgrave Macmillan, 2011.

———. *Preparing Successors for Leadership: Another Kind of Hero*. New York: Palgrave Macmillan, 2010.

———. *Preparing Your Family Business for Strategic Change*. New York: Palgrave Macmillan, 2010.

Astrachan, Joseph H., and Kristi S. McMillan. *Conflict and Communication in the Family Business*. Marietta, GA: Family Enterprise Publishers, 2003.

Bennedsen, Morton, and Joseph P.H. Fan. *The Family Business Map: Assets and Roadblocks in Long-Term Planning*. New York: Palgrave Macmillan, 2014.

Berger, Warren. *A More Beautiful Question: The Power of Inquiry to Spark Breakthrough Ideas*. New York: Bloomsbury, 2014.

Block, Peter. *Flawless Consulting: A Guide to Getting Your Expertise Used*. San Francisco, CA: Pfeiffer, 2011.

Bork, David, Dennis T. Jaffe, Sam H. Lane, Leslie Dashew, and Quentin G. Heisler. *Working with Family Businesses: A Guide for Professionals*. San Francisco, CA: Jossey-Bass Inc., 1996.

Carlock, Randel S., and John L. Ward. *Strategic Planning for the Family Business: Parallel Planning to Unify the Family and Business*. New York: Palgrave, 2001.

———. *When Family Businesses Are Best: The Parallel Planning Process for Family Harmony and Business Success*. New York: Palgrave Macmillan, 2010.

Collins, Jim. *Good to Great: Why Some Companies Make the Leap and Others Don't*. New York: HarperCollins, 2001.

Collins, Jim, and Jerry I. Porras. *Built to Last: Successful Habits of Visionary Companies*. New York: HarperBusiness, 2002.

de Visscher, François M., Craig E. Aronoff, and John L. Ward. *Financing Transitions: Managing Capital and Liquidity in the Family Business*. New York: Palgrave Macmillan, 2011.

Dickinson, Arlene. *Persuasion: A New Approach to Changing Minds*. Toronto: HarperCollins Canada, 2011.

Eckrich, Christopher J., and Stephen L. McClure. *Working for a Family Business: A Non-Family Employee's Guide to Success*. New York: Palgrave Macmillan, 2011.

Fleming, Quentin J. *Keep the Family Baggage out of the Family Business:*

Avoiding the Seven Deadly Sins that Destroy Family Businesses. New York: Simon & Schuster, 2000.

Frankenberg, Ellen. *Your Family, Inc.: Practical Tips for Building a Healthy Family Business.* Philadelphia: The Haworth Press, 1999.

Gutsche, Jeremy. *Exploiting Chaos: 150 Ways to Spark Innovation during Times of Change.* New York: Penguin Group, 2009.

Hausner, Lee. *Children of Paradise: Successful Parenting for Prosperous Families.* Los Angeles: Tarcher, 1990.

Hess, Edward D. *The Successful Family Business: A Proactive Plan for Managing the Family and the Business.* Westport, CT: Praeger Publishers, 2006.

Hilburt-Davis, Jane, and W. Gibb Dyer, Jr. *Consulting to Family Businesses: A Practical Guide to Contracting, Assessment, and Implementation.* San Francisco: Pfeiffer, 2003.

Hughes, James E., Jr. *Family: The Compact Among Generations: Answers and Insights from a Lifetime of Helping Families Flourish.* Hoboken, NJ: Bloomberg Press, 2007.

———. *Family Wealth: Keeping It in the Family.* Hoboken, NJ: Bloomberg Press, 2004.

Hughes, James E., Susan E. Massenzio, and Keith Whitaker. *The Cycle of a Gift: Family Wealth and Wisdom.* Hoboken, NJ: Bloomberg Press, 2013.

Kahneman, Daniel. *Thinking, Fast and Slow.* Toronto: Anchor Canada, 2013.

Kaslow, Florence W. *Handbook of Family Business and Family Business Consultation: A Global Perspective.* New York: Haworth Press, 2006.

Kenyon-Rouvinez, Denise H., Gordon Adler, Guido Corbetta, and Gianfilippo Cuneo. *Sharing Wisdom, Building Values: Letters from Family Business Owners to Their Successors.* Marietta, GA: Family Enterprise Publishers, 2002.

Kenyon-Rouvinez, Denise, and John L. Ward. *Family Business Key Issues.* New York: Palgrave Macmillan, 2005.

Keyt, Andrew. *Myths & Mortals: Family Business Leadership and Succession Planning.* Hoboken, New Jersey: John Wiley & Sons, Inc. 2015.

Kyle, Mackenzie. *Making It Happen: A Non-Technical Guide to Project Management.* Ontario: John Wiley & Sons Canada, Ltd., 1998.

———. *The Performance Principle: A Practical Guide to Understanding Motivation in the Modern Workplace.* Vancouver: Figure 1 Publishing, 2016.

Lansberg, Ivan. *Succeeding Generations: Realizing the Dreams of Families in Business*. Boston, MA: Harvard Business School Press, 1999.

Latremoille, Susan, et al. *On the Shoulders of Atlas: A Story about Transitioning a Family-Owned Business*. Toronto: The Latremoille Group, 2010.

Leman, Kevin. *The Birth Order Book: Why You Are the Way You Are*. Grand Rapids, MI: Revell, 2009.

Lencioni, Patrick. *Five Dysfunctions of a Team: A Leadership Fable*. San Francisco: Jossey-Bass, 2002.

Lewis, Michael. *The Undoing Project: A Friendship that Changed our Minds*. New York: W. W. Norton & Company, 2017.

Lipton, Bruce H. *The Biology of Belief: Unleashing the Power of Consciousness, Matter and Miracles*. New York: Hay House, Inc. 2015.

Lucas, Stuart E. Wealth: *Grow It, Protect It, Spend It, and Share It*. Philadelphia, PA: Wharton School Publishing, 2008.

Lucy, Robb. *Legacies Aren't Just for Dead People! Discover Happiness and a Meaningful Life by Creating and Enjoying Your Legacies – Now!* Canada: Engage Communications Inc., 2015.

Minuchin, Salvador, and H. Charles Fishman. *Family Therapy Techniques*. Cambridge, Mass. and London, Eng.: Harvard University Press, 1981.

Mlodinow, Leonard. *Subliminal: How Your Unconscious Mind Rules Your Behavior*. New York: Random House, Inc., 2012.

Montemerlo, Daniela, and John L. Ward. *The Family Constitution: Agreements to Secure and Perpetuate Your Family and Your Business*. New York: Palgrave Macmillan, 2011.

Nanus, Burt. *Visionary Leadership: Creating a Compelling Sense of Direction for Your Organization*. San Francisco: Jossey-Bass Publishers, 1992.

Perry, Ann. *The Wise Inheritor: Protecting, Preserving, and Enjoying Your Legacy*. New York: Broadway Books, 2003.

Rafferty, Renata J. *Don't Just Give It Away: How to Make the Most of Your Charitable Giving*. Worcester, MA: Chandler House Press, 1999.

Renkert-Thomas, Amelia. *Engaged Ownership: A Guide for Owners of Family Businesses*. New Jersey: John Wiley & Sons, Inc., 2016.

Richardson, Ronald W. *Family Ties that Bind: A Guide to Change through Family of Origin Therapy*. Canada: International Self-Counsel Press Ltd., 2014.

Rosenberg, Marshall B. *Nonviolent Communication*. Encinitas, CA: PuddleDancer Press, 2003.

Rosplock, Kirby. *The Complete Family Office Handbook: A Guide for Affluent Families and the Advisors Who Serve Them.* Hoboken, New Jersey: John Wiley & Sons, Inc., 2014.

Schuman, Amy M., *Nurturing the Talent to Nurture the Legacy: Career Development in the Family Business.* Marietta, GA: Family Enterprise Publishers, 2004.

Schuman, Amy M., and John L. Ward. *Family Education for Business-Owning Families: Strengthening Bonds by Learning Together.* New York: Palgrave Macmillan, 2011.

Sellery, Bruce. *Moolala: Why Smart People Do Dumb Things with Their Money (and What You Can Do About It).* Toronto: McClelland & Stewart Ltd., 2011.

Syed, Matthew. *Black Box Thinking: The Surprising Truth About Success (And Why Some People Never Learn From Their Mistakes).* London: John Murray, 2015.

Taleb, Nassim Nicholas. *Antifragile: Things That Gain from Disorder.* New York: Random House, 2014.

Tatum, Doug. *No Man's Land: Where Growing Companies Fail.* New York: Penguin Group, 2008.

Treliving, Jim. *Decisions: Making the Right Ones, Righting the Wrong Ones.* Toronto: HarperCollins Canada, 2012.

Ward, John L. *Creating Effective Boards for Private Enterprises: Meeting the Challenges of Continuity and Competition.* San Francisco: Jossey-Bass Publishers, 1991.

——. *Keeping the Family Business Healthy: How to Plan for Continuing Growth, Profitability, and Family Leadership.* New York: Palgrave Macmillan, 2011.

——. *Perpetuating the Family Business: 50 Lessons Learned from Long-Lasting, Successful Families in Business.* New York: Palgrave Macmillan, 2004.

Whiteside, Mary F., Craig E. Aronoff, and John L. Ward. *How Families Work Together.* New York: Palgrave Macmillan, 2011.

Williams, Roy O. *Preparing Your Family to Manage Wealth: A Comprehensive Guide to Estate and Succession Planning, and to Building a Family Team.* Marina, CA: Monterey Pacific Institute, 1992.

Williams, Roy, and Vic Preisser. *Philanthropy, Heirs and Values: How Successful Families are Using Philanthropy to Prepare Their Heirs for Post-Transition Responsibilities.* Bandon, OR: Robert D. Reed Publishers, 2005.

——. *Preparing Heirs: Five Steps to a Successful Transition of Family Wealth and Values.* Bandon, OR: Robert D. Reed Publishers, 2003.

Willis, Thayer C. *Navigating the Dark Side of Wealth: A Life Guide for Inheritors.* Portland, OR: New Concord Press, 2003.

Zander, Rosamund Stone, and Benjamin Zander. *The Art of Possibility: Transforming Professional and Personal Life.* New York: Penguin Books, 2002.

CORPORATE PUBLICATIONS

BDO Dunwoody LLP. *Succession Planning for the Family Farm,* 2007. Accessed at: bdo.ca/library/publications/tax/taxbulletins/012007.cfm.

Credit Suisse Group. *Life After an Exit: How Entrepreneurs Transition to the Next Stage.* Entrepreneurs White Paper 03, The Eugene Lang Entrepreneurship Center, Columbia Business School, 2011.

Ernst & Young Family Business Center for Excellence. *Built to Last: Family Businesses Lead the Way to Sustainable Growth.* EYGM Ltd., 2012.

——. *Coming Home or Breaking Free? Career Choice Intentions of the Next Generation in Family Businesses.* EYGM Ltd., 2012.

——. *Succeeding for Generations.* EYGM Ltd., 2011.

Johnson, Howard E. *Selling Your Private Company: The Value Enhancement Framework for Business Owners.* Veracap Corporate Finance Limited, 2005.

KPMG Enterprise. *Constructing a Family Constitution.* KPMG, 2011.

——. *Family Business Matters.* KPMG, 2012.

——. *Family Business Succession: Managing the All-Important Family Component.* KPMG, 2011.

——. *Keeping It in the Family: Governance for Family Business.* KPMG, 2011.

——. *Family Ties: Canadian Business in the Family Way.* KPMG, 2012.

Kruger, Sarah, and Sean Foran. *Succession Stories from the Front Line: Insights and Advice for Canadian Business Owners.* Bank of Montreal, 2008.

PwC Family Business Services. *Making a Difference: The Pricewaterhouse Coopers Family Business Survey 2007/08.* PwC, 2007.

Walsh, Grant. *Family Business Succession: Managing: The All-Important Family Component.* KPMG, 2011.

PODCASTS

Art of Charm: Only Episodes #692 and earlier, specifically:

———, Episode #385. Chris Taylor, *Deliberate Choice: Going Beyond the Picket Fence* (March 16, 2015) (available at theartofcharm. com/?s=385).

———, Episode #463. Jeff Goins, *How to Find Your Calling* (November 22, 2015) (available at theartofcharm.com/?s=463).

———, Episode #519. Ryan Holiday, *Ego Is the Enemy* (June 6, 2016) (available at theartofcharm.com/?s=519).

———, Episode #573. General Stanley McChrystal, *New Rules of Engagement* (December 12, 2016) (available at theartofcharm.com/?s=573).

———, Episode #612. Andy Molinsky, *A Reach from Comfort* (April 26, 2017) (available at theartofcharm.com/?s=612).

———, Episode #645: Richard Clarke, *Warnings, Cassandras, and Catastrophes* (August 21, 2017) (available at theartofcharm.com/?s=645).

Bulletproof Radio. *Peter Sage: Entrepreneurship, Starting a Business, & How to Break Bad Habits* (September 11, 2015) (available at youtube. com/watch?v=QLHb5kzY4sU).

———, #275. Dave Asprey, *Stella Grizont: The Work Happiness Method* (n.d.) (available at blog.bulletproof.com/stella-grizont-the-work-happiness-method-275/).

Freakonomics. Stephen J. Dubner, *Trust Me* (November 10, 2016) (available at freakonomics.com/podcast/trust-me).

TED NPR Radio Hour. *Trust and Consequences* (May 15, 2016) (available at https://www.npr.org/programs/ted-radio-hour/406238794/trust-and-consequences).

ONLINE RESOURCES

Chiner, Alfonso, and Josep Tapias Lloret. "Top 10 Tips for Good Governance." Posting on IESEinsight.com. Accessed March 14, 2012, at ieseinsight.com/docImpression.aspx?id=00767

Duckworth, Angela. angeladuckworth.com

FamilyBusinessWiki.org. Postings on family business topics, including "Deferred Compensation," "Enmeshed Families," "Governance," "Stewardship," and "Strategic Planning for the Family Business." Accessed March 14, 2012, at familybusinesswiki.org

Hughes, James E., Jr. "Articles and Reflections." A collection of writings available on Family Matters: The Official Website of James E. Hughes, Jr., at jameshughes.com/articles.php

Hutcheson, James Olan. "Building a Board of Directors: When is the Right Time?" Blog posting on FamilyBusinessWiki.org. January 31, 2013. Accessed March 6, 2013, at familybusinesswiki.ning.com/profiles/blogs/building-a-board-of-directors-when-is-the-right-time

———. "Hidden Hurdles in Healing Families." Blog posting on FamilyBusinessWiki.org, January 31, 2013. Accessed March 6, 2013, at familybusinesswiki.ning.com/profiles/blogs/hidden-hurdles-in-healing-families

Ward, John L. "The Ten Subtle Secrets of Successful Family Businesses." Blog posting on FamilyBusinessWiki.org, December 20, 2009. Accessed June 7, 2012, at familybusinesswiki.ning.com/profiles/blogs/the-ten-subtle-secrets-of

FROM THE WEBSITE OF THE FAMILY BUSINESS CONSULTING GROUP (THEFBCG.COM)

No authors ascribed

"A Family Employment Policy Answers Questions." "A Flexible Response to Unanswered Questions." "A Non-Family Exec Worries About the Future." "Active Owners Explain Family's Commitment to Employees." "AFLAC Prospers under Family Leadership." "Appraising Boardroom Performance." "Are You Listening?" "Assuring Financial Freedom." "Attitudes Critical for Sibling Success." "Balancing Inside and Outside Stockholders Needs." "Best Practices for Managing Key Non-Family Executives." "Bundle of Sticks." "Business Owners: Provide Yourself a Secure Financial Future." "Business Valuations: A Family Business Tool." "Can We Pledge Our Shares?" "Chair/CEO Roles Increasingly Separate." "Challenges in Captivating the Next Generations: How to Create Interest among Teens." "Changing Attitudes Toward Family Business Finance." "Chomping at the Bit." "Choose to be Happy." "Choosing to Sell Your Shares." "Co-Leaders: A Cop-Out on the Part of Parents of Sibling Owners, or a Sound Leadership Model?" "Commitment Saves Jolly Time." "Common Independent Director Assumptions." "Compensating Your Board of Directors." "Confidentiality in the Information Age." "Considering a Sale of the Family Business?" "Content of a Family Constitution." "Criteria for Evaluating the Board." "Culture, Strategy and Execution Drive Enterprise." "Dealing with Frustrations." "Developing a Philosophy of Compensation." "Directors of Private Company Found Liable in Bankruptcy Suit." "Don't Complain about Siblings to Spouses." "Don't Just Build

Business, Build Your Organization." "Economic or Emotional Deci-
sions." "Economist Says: Private Ownership Is Better." "Employment
Policy Allows Family Buy-Out." "Engaging in Learning about the
Business: Insight from a Fifth-Generation Family Member." "Ensure
Successful Sibling Partnerships: Three Dimensions." "Establishing
an Effective Board." "Even if Dad Won't Let Go, Siblings Should Pre-
pare for the Future." "Fair Process So Important, So Subtle." "Family
Business or Family Glue?" "Family Businesses and Shareholder Value."
"Family Communism/Business Capitalism." "Family Fingers in the
Till." "Family Goals: The Beginning and the End." "Family Members
as Employees." "Family Reunions and Annual Meetings." "Family
Shareholder Liquidity." "Finding Fault." "From Control to Account-
ability." "Funding Family Needs Can Build Commitment." "Giving
Stock to Employees." "Grappling with Complexity and Uncertainty."
"Healthy Motivations for Family Business Succession." "Hitting the
Wall on Growth." "How Boards Serve Owners' Goals." "How Do I Bring
My Son Back to the Business?" "How Do We Deal with Entitlement?
Or Can We Learn Anything from Illinois Governor Rod Blagojevich?"
"How Effective Is Your Board." "How Strong is Your Family?" "How to
Promote Change By . . . Reinterpreting Traditions." "How to Protect
Your Business in a Divorce Action." "How to Succeed as a Non-CEO
Family Business." "In and Out of the Business: Gifting Fairly." "In
New Economy or Old: Defining and Living Excellence is the Key." "In-
Law Loses Marriage, Keeps Job." "Investment Strategies for Business
Owners." "It's Not Just Economics." "Job Performance and Family
Peace." "Keeping Family in the Family Meeting." "Keeping the Family
and Business Together." "Leading and Ending with Charity." "Leading
Family Members in the Business." "Lessons on Ownership from the
Sale of Knight Ridder." "Linking Family and Business Governance
in Later Generations." "Losing Control Through Family Meetings."
"Machiavelli's The Prince." "Making Loans to Children." "Making Sib-
ling Teams Work." "Managing Owner Expectations about Sitting on
Boards." "Mission Statements for Cousin Clans." "Money is Plentiful:
What Easy Credit Means to Family Firms." "Motivating Stock Gift-
ing." "Next Generation Leaders: Don't Throw the Baby Out with the
Bathwater." "Nuptial Agreements: How Do I Love Thee?" "Outsiders:
Troublemakers or Truth Tellers." "Ownership Matters." "Part 2: Party
Time." "Piggy Bank." "Policies for Moving into the Second Generation."
"Preparing for a Divorce." "Preparing the Board for a Non-Family CEO."
"Qualifications of Directors." "Reducing the Risks of Family-Business

Growth." "Reimbursement of Travel Expenses for Family Meetings." "Resisting Manipulation." "R-E-S-P-E-C-T." "Secrecy — A Family Business Vice?" "Security for Ex-Spouses." "Share Philosophy Makes Practical Decisions Smoother." "Should an In-law Become CEO?" "Should I Leave the Family Business?" "Sibling Code of Conduct." "Socializing with Employees." "Sources of Conflict: Family Business 'Hot Spots.'" "Sticking by Family Business Policies." "Straight Talk on Succession Planning." "Strengthening the Family Business Culture." "Structuring Your Company for Change." "Succession with Non-Descriptive Expectations." "Talking About Wealth." "The Balanced Scorecard, Revisited." "The Birds Always Sing After the Rain." "The Burdens of Ownership." "The Disinheritors." "The Family Business Golden Rule: Open and Honest Communication." "The Family Factor in Family Business — Does Your Family Add or Subtract." "The Imperial Trustee: Whose Money Is It?" "The IPO Itch: When Consolidations Come Calling." "The Job Description of Mom." "The Psychology of Wealth." "The Transformation of a Tradition." "Think As a Clan for Long-Term Success." "To Be or Not To Be: Should an In-Law Join the Family Business?" "Trust Me, or Else." "Trust: The Basis of Family Business Advantage." "Understanding Roles and Responsibilities." "Values Dilemmas." "Values Dilemmas (Part II)." "What Does Non-Family Management Want From Ownership?" "What is the Definition of Family." "What Should an Employment Policy Contain?" "What to Look for in a Non-Family CEO." "What to Think about Before Joining Your Family's Business." "What's a Father to Do?" "When a Man Marries the Boss." "When an Owner is Fired." "When Can Family Members Serve on the Board?" "When Does the Board Get Involved in 'Vision'?" "Who Belongs on a Family Council." "Whose Fault is Failure." "Why Don't More Family Firms Have Independent Directors." "Winning with Ownership Team Defense."

Specific Authors

Aronoff, Craig E. "A Chairman Defines His Role." "Family Business Fosters Long-Term Innovation." "Family Business Is No Excuse." "Family Business Leadership and Values Shaped Atlanta's Future." "Family Commitment Yields Transition Success." "Family Guidelines for a Business Board." "Five Questions to Help You Think About Joining the Family Business." "How to Get a Family Business Career Back on Track Following a Disappointing Start." "How to Transition from a Family-Run to a Family-Owned Business."

"'Letting Go' is a Two-Way Street." "Pre-Mortem Beats Post-Mortem." "Questions Can Ease Generational Transitions." "Record Your History — Before It's Too Late." "Should our Kids Have Summer Jobs When Employees Have Been Laid Off?" "Standards for Evaluating Family Business Practice and Behavior." "Ten Strategic Questions for the Next Generation." "Three Family Keys to Multi-Generational Business Success." "Transitioning the Board for a New Generation." "You Don't Have to Retire (But Is Hanging On Worth the Price?)"

Aronoff, Craig E., Joseph H. Astrachan, and John L. Ward. "Family Business Policies: Why You Need Them."

Aronoff, Craig E., Drew S. Mendoza, and John L. Ward. "Building a Healthy Team."

Aronoff, Craig E., and John L. Ward. "An Open Letter to the Non-Family Executive." "Are You an Owner by Choice?" "Empowering the Next Generation with the Future." "How Outgoing CEO's Can Make Change a Tradition." "How Successful Business Families Get That Way." "Optimizing Ownership: Values, Vision, Goals." "Owners By Choice." "Policy-Making: The Process." "Set Policies Now to Solve Future Problems." "Sibling Teams: Understanding the Emotional Problems." "Summer Jobs for Family."

Baskin, Otis W. "Governance Beats Avoidance for Long-Term Family Business Harmony." "What Happens After You Succeed?"

Brun de Pontet, Stephanie. "Addressing the Fears that Come with Succession." "Planting the First Seeds of Family Business Education." "Seeking the Gold: Striving for Balance while Delivering Peak Performance in the Family Business." "Should I Call You Dad? (And Other Perils of Working for Your Family Business...)."

Brun de Pontet, Stephanie, and John Ward. "The Case for Clarity on Future Ownership."

Dartt, Barbara, and Anne Hargrave. "Getting Started with Family Governance."

Echrich, Christopher, and Stephen McClure. "Understanding the Differences Among Family Governance Forums."

Eckrich, Chris, and Stephen McClure. "15 Lessons Family Councils Wish They Knew Before They Started." "A Family Council: A Renegotiation of Relationships." "Building the Best Team Possible: Relationships Between Family and Non-Family Employees." "Decision Making on Family Business Matters." "Employing Family Members as Vendors and Supplier." "Family Perks: Benefit or

Boondoggle?" "Sharing Family Cottages, Lodges and Resorts: Part 1." "Should Spouses Work in the Family Business?" "To Select or To Elect? Decision-Making Methods for Family Member Roles in Family and Business Governance." "Toward Greater Objectivity on Your Board." "What do Family Councils Do?"

Eckrich, Christopher, Michael Fassler, and Wendy Sage-Hayward. "Understanding Profitability in the Family Business."

Eckrich, Christopher, and Bernard Kliska. "Fighting the Family Feuds."

Eckrich, Christopher, Stephen McClure, and Ross Nager. "Sharing Family Resorts, Cottages and Lodges: Part 2."

Eckrich, Christopher J. "Business Wisdom for the Family." "Family Employment Policies: Best Practices." "It's a Matter of Trust." "Letting Go, Stepping Up: Leadership in Transition."

Eckrich, Christopher J., and Amy Schuman. "Accountability in Family Governance: A Key Variable for Building Trust." "How Can We Have More Accountability in Our Family Business?"

Fassler, Michael, and Wendy Sage-Hayward. "Managing Risk in the Family Enterprise: It's More than Financial." "Risk Management Conversation Starter."

Fassler, Mike. "Accountability in the Family Business: Creating a Culture for Success."

Houden, Deb. "How to Manage Chronic Conflict in Your Family Enterprise."

Houden, Deb, and Wendy Sage-Hayward. "Undiscussables: Dealing with the Elephants in Family Business."

Johnson, Barry, Amy Schuman, and John Ward. "Mastering Family Business Polarities: Learning to Manage Dilemmas That Can't Be Solved."

Kliska, Bernard. "After the Disaster: Rebuild, Retool or Retire?" "Bringing in Fresh Air: Using a Board of Advisors." "Bringing Stepfamilies into the Family Business." "Death and the Family Business." "Enhance Communication and Avoiding Misunderstandings." "Firing a Family Member." "Honoring Family Traditions in a Changing World." "Teaching Wealthy Children About Wealth." "To Sell or Not Sell: That is the Question." "Wealth and Children: Being Successful with Both." "Welcoming a Child into the Family Business."

Kliska, Bernard, and Amy Schuman. "Planning a Funeral for Your Family Business."

Lansky, David. "Family Meetings: Some Guidelines." "Managing the Psychological Impact of Inherited Wealth." "Men, Women, and Money." "Money and Meaning: Planning for the Next Generation." "Silence Is Golden ... Sometimes."

Lansky, David, and Amy Schuman. "Achieving Balance: Individual Rights and Family Interest."

LeCouvie, Kelly. "Conditions for the Successful Management of BIG Change." "The Leverage of Kindness." "The Non-Strategic Value of Directors." "A Planning Guide for Transforming Your Company's Board of Directors."

LeCouvie, Kelly, and Jennifer Pendergast. "Don't Think of It as 'Succession Planning'..."

McClure, Stephen. "Filling a Board Vacancy: Using Gap Analysis to Capture Opportunities." "Find the Best Independent Directors for Your Family Business." "Getting Non-Operating Shareholders Appropriately Involved." "How to Succeed in a Family Business." "Next Generation Development with a Mentor Team." "Leadership of a Family Council: Directive Leader or Servant Leader?" "Scheduling Family Meetings: A Surprising Lightening Rod for Family Conflict." "Should We Separate the Chair and CEO Roles in Our Family Business?"

McClure, Stephen, and Jennifer Pendergast. "Transitioning from Family Leadership to Non-Family CEO: Best Practices for Maintaining a Family Enterprise."

Mendoza, Drew. "Adult Siblings in Family Business: Dreams Defer to Reality." "Family Meetings: A Three Legged Stool."

Miller, Stephen P. "Developing Next-Generation Leaders in Family Business." "Shared Vision and Effective Next-Generation Leaders: Two Sides of the Same Coin."

Nacht, Joshua. "Family Champions: Energy for Success."

Nager, Ross. "Parting Ways — Part 2: The Valuation Conundrum." "Parting Ways — Part 3: The Value Equations." "Parting Ways — Part 4: Let My People Go." "Shareholder Agreements — Parting Ways: Part 1."

Norton, JoAnne. "Creating Win-Wins for Non-Family Executives." "Family Councils: Who Needs Them?" "Seven Steps to Sustainability in Family Business — A Cautionary Tale." "Ten Rules for Successful CEOs in Family Firms."

Pendergast, Jennifer M. "Capital Markets and Family Business: Some Surprising Results." "Creating Successful Decision Making Groups." "Family Business Boards: Demystifying the Process." "Getting the Most Out of Your Board." "How Board Evaluations Drive the Planning Process." "How Sophisticated Does Our Governance Need to Be?" "How to Make Strategic Planning Successful." "Leading the Board: Qualities of an Effective Chair." "Owners' Discussion on Selling the Business." "Report Cards as a Family Business Tool." "The Myths About Family Business Growth." "The Right Reasons to Sell." "We Need a Policy for Hiring Members of 3G." "What It Means To Be an Investing Owner and Why It's So Important." "Why Family Business Owners Need a Job Description."

Pendergast, Jennifer M., and Amy Schuman. "Rotational Systems: An Approach to Career Development."

Rhodes, Kent. "Advice to the Next Generation from Their 'Elders.'" "Keeping Conflict in Play or at Bay? Old Habits Play a Role in Family Business." "Putting Coaching to Work in the Family Business." "Six Keys to Successful Family Foundation Creation."

Rhodes, Kent, and Dana Telford. "Emotional Ownership."

Schmieder, Joe. "Evolving Your Family Business Board."

Schmieder, Joe, and John L. Ward. "Succession Suggestions from India."

Schuman, Amy M. "Biggest Reason for Not Holding Family Meetings." "Family Education: Perfect is the Enemy of Good." "Family Employment and Career Guidance: One Size Does Not Fit All." "Going to Work in the Family Business." "Honoring Both Family and Business Considerations in Compensation Approaches." "Successful Ownership Transitions Rest on Strong, Knowledgeable Shareholders." "The 80/20 Rule: Balancing Ownership and Management Responsibilities." "Tough Economic Times Put Family Businesses to the Test."

Schuman, Amy, and Stephanie Brun de Pontet. "Mindfulness Brings Calm, Compassion and Creativity to Family Enterprises."

Schwartz, Norbert. "Family Business Loan Programs." "Musings on the Roles of Parents and Business Successors." "Useful Questions to Inform Strategic Planning."

Telford, Dana. "From Partners by Chance to Partners by Choice: The 7 Cs of Trust-based Partnerships."

Ward, John L. "Commencement." "Conflicts of Interest." "Directors Ask: What's My Role." "Family Foundation as Family Glue."

"Harnessing the Power of Your Board." "Helping a Smart Board Also Be Wise." "Maximizing the Board's Value." "Supporting the Successor." "Ten Myths About Outside Boards." "The New Capitalism and Family Enterprise." "The Roles and Responsibilities of Family Ownership." "The Succession Task Force: A Tool for Managing Challenging Times." "Voice and Exit in the Family Firm." "When Should Spouses Attend Sibling Meetings?"

ACKNOWLEDGMENTS

IT IS my unwavering opinion that a list like this is never complete. So, for anyone I may have unintentionally missed, please know that all your efforts and contributions were much appreciated. Thank you all for your insights, support and encouragement.

This book would not exist without the efforts and experiences of the families I have worked alongside. These are the families who have demonstrated compassion for their fellow family members as they worked together on a shared journey to benefit not only the current but also future generations. With each family I meet, I am consistently inspired by the power of one—one united family, their genuine caring and concern for one another and their determination to work through the theories of this subject matter in order to make it their own. I am humbled and truly grateful to have been a part of these families' shared journeys.

Having been supported in the publication of my first book by successful, smart, contemplative business builders, like Randy Shaw, John Bowe, Leanne Bate, George Noroian, Darcy Kernighan, Rob Hartvikson and Donald Mackenzie, I received the priceless gift of encouragement to push on and write this companion book to *Build Your Family Bank*.

To the team I work alongside—which has expanded from my first book from John Gjervan, Lynn Delahey and Maggie Lui to also include Karen Lau, Allison Fulton, Kyla Foley and Peter Kaye—thank you all for your commitment and dedication to remaining focused on putting the needs of our clients and their family enterprises first.

Another individual I work closely with and want to thank is Gary Brookes. I know I can always turn to you for wise counsel, delivered with grace and insight.

Gary Nott, you played a key role in the genesis of this book, just as you did in the first one. In one of our conversations about family businesses and family enterprises, you suggested that I should create a research library for my clients based on my research and practical findings. It is this work that became the backbone of this book. Thank you, Gary.

Ken Ingo and Fred Withers, you were my first bosses in public accounting decades ago. Thank you for taking a chance on a very young person and role-modeling for me right from the start what good leadership looks and sounds like. I am forever grateful that I chose to join Ernst & Young (formerly Clarkson Gordon) and even more grateful you allowed me to join your team.

To Linda Hamer, Ruth Steverlynck, Grant Smith, Don Breen, David Coe and Bruce Sellery, thank you for actively listening and sharing ideas with me. I am grateful for your genuine ongoing support and encouragement of my work.

Vladimir Simokovickeller, who brings a smile to my face just in writing his name, flew from Zurich to London, UK, to meet with me after reading my first book. We subsequently struck up a cross-global idea-vetting friendship. When I isolated myself for several months to write this book, Vladi played a key role in keeping me motivated to finish it by sharing his valuable time and knowledge during lengthy multi-time-zone telephone calls. His enthusiasm for the ideas in this book further encouraged me to completion. Thank you, Vladi.

To Suzy Mayhew, and the team at Campden Wealth, thank you for reaching out to me, supporting my work and allowing me to share my work and strategies with families from across the globe. As a keen supporter of Campden Wealth, I am grateful for the work you do for family businesses and family enterprises. I am proud to be a part of your journey.

To Claire Barry, this companion book to my first one would likely not exist today without the extraordinary attention my first "unknown book" by an "unknown author" received because of your work as a media consultant. Thank you, Claire, for your time, expertise and hours spent arranging, and then attending with me, media interviews. You are a marvel.

James (Jay) E. Hughes Jr. is the author of *Family Wealth: Keeping it in the Family*—and someone I was in awe of. I regarded him as a rockstar in the arena of considered transitions of family wealth. Sometimes people are disappointed when they meet their rockstars, because their expectations were so high. This was not the case for me. My path crossed with Jay's on a professional basis after the publication of my first book. His support not only for *Build Your Family Bank* but also for my writing this book has meant more to me than he could ever possibly know. Thank you, Jay.

To the team at Figure 1 Publishing, including Chris Labonté, Lara Smith and Jessica Sullivan, I am profoundly aware of how lucky I am to be in your capable, calm and professional hands. The guidance and direction I have received from the entire team at Figure 1 has been invaluable. Thank you to you all!

I was also exceedingly fortunate to find myself in the hands of the same substantive editor, Barbara Pulling, as I had on my first book. Yet again, she masterfully, and kindly, transformed my writing from compressed carbon into a clear-cut diamond.

I don't know how she does it, but I'm forever grateful. Thank you, Barbara.

Lesley Cameron and Renate Preuss, as copy editor and proofreader respectively, worked to ensure every line and thought in this book was clear and accurate. Thank you, Lesley and Renate.

Elise Rees, a recently retired tax partner from Ernst & Young and a longtime friend, your ongoing support for and curiosity about what it is I specifically do for families and family enterprises helps to focus me each and every time I work with family members. Thank you, Elise.

To my lake neighbors and friends, Bruce Barclay and Julie and Brian Welch, thank you for your ongoing support for my writing efforts and your always warm and inviting open-door policy. In fact, on the day I finished my first draft of this book, I happened to wander across the threshold of Julie and Brian's cabin. Thank you for welcoming me in to celebrate this achievement with your family and friends.

Thank you, Gill Kassell, for your decades-long friendship, and also for teaching me the art of joy and celebration when all I can see is the work and struggles ahead and that there is always a good reason for a champagne toast.

To Lorine Bowe, no matter how near or far apart we are, thank you for always being there for me and for being a strong vocal supporter of my work.

At every corner and every turn, one can only hope to find a friend like Monica, full of grace, serenity and wisdom. I know how extraordinarily fortunate I am that no matter the time of day or what exactly I need, I can turn to Monica and she will offer the necessary insights, kindness and wisdom, all the while being both honest and supportive.

To my late mother-in-law, Geraldine; my father-in-law, George; brothers-in-law, Neal and Jeff; and sister-in-law, Sheryl, all of you respected community leaders and farmers in a shared family business, thank you for keeping it real and fun. I am thankful you welcomed me with open arms into your family.

It almost goes without saying that I must acknowledge my grandparents and parents, for their visions for our family enterprise, and also my siblings, for a lifetime of remarkable experiences. Most specifically, though, I want to acknowledge my first business partner and brother, Arthur, for inviting me to share in a family business and family enterprise journey with him decades ago and for being so utterly supportive of my work today. A sister couldn't ask for a better brother!

To my sons, David and Brandon, as you continue to mature into young men leading purposeful independent lives, as a mother I couldn't be any prouder. I am so grateful you allow me to share in your journeys.

Paul, you are my husband, my best friend and the person I admire and respect most. Day after day, you support me every step of the way. None of this work would have been possible without you by my side. When I married you, I won the real lottery of life.

INDEX

ABOUT
THE AUTHOR

EMILY GRIFFITHS-HAMILTON is a chartered accountant, a
family enterprise advisor, and a conflict resolution coach who
brings three generations of experience to the subject of wealth
and family-business transition planning. Her maternal grandfather, veterinarian Dr. William Ballard, was one of North
America's greatest dynamic wealth creators. Her father, Frank
A. Griffiths, FCA, built a highly successful sports and media
empire. Griffiths-Hamilton herself has been the co-owner
of a National Hockey League team, the Vancouver Canucks; a
National Basketball Association franchise, the Vancouver Grizzlies; and a state-of-the-art arena.

Griffiths-Hamilton's professional training, expertise and
unique first-hand experience have given her a deep understanding of the benefits of clear, considered succession and
family business transition planning. Today, she is passionate about advising individuals and families on the effective,
responsible transition of wealth and family businesses over
generations. Her first book, *Build Your Family Bank: A Winning
Vision for Multigenerational Wealth*, was released in 2014.

www.buildyourfamilybank.com